Mamá

Mamá

LATINA DAUGHTERS
CELEBRATE THEIR MOTHERS

Maria Perez-Brown

Photographs by Julie Bidwell

An Imprint of HarperCollinsPublishers

MAMÁ. Copyright © 2003 by Maria Perez-Brown. All rights reserved.
Printed in the United States of America. No part of this book may be used or
reproduced in any manner whatsoever without written permission except in the
case of brief quotations embodied in critical articles and reviews. For information,
address HarperCollins Publishers Inc., 10 East 53rd Street, New York, NY 10022.

HarperCollins books may be purchased for educational, business, or sales
promotional use. For information, please write: Special Markets Department,
HarperCollins Publishers Inc., 10 East 53rd Street, New York, NY 10022.

Photographs of the Saraleguis on pages 192–198 © 2003 by Pablo Blum.

FIRST EDITION

DESIGNED BY JUDITH STAGNITTO ABBATE / ABBATE DESIGN

Printed on acid-free paper

Library of Congress Cataloging-in-Publication Data
Perez-Brown, Maria
Mamá : Latina daughters celebrate their mothers / by Maria Perez-Brown ;
photographs by Julie Bidwell.—1st ed.
p.   cm.
ISBN 0-06-008386-7
1. Hispanic American women—Family relationships. 2. Mothers and daughters—
United States. I. Bidwell, Julie II. Title.
E184.S75 P464 2003
306.874'3'08968073—dc21   2002037032

03   04   05   06   07   DIX/QW   10   9   8   7   6   5   4   3   2   1

To my mother, Juana Grajales,

and to my sisters, Luz Thomas and Gladys Perez Johnson,

for their love, friendship, and support

CONTENTS

ACKNOWLEDGMENTS

I WANT TO THANK my husband, Keith Michael Brown, for his unconditional love, guidance, and encouragement every step of the way. I will always cherish you. It was while traveling around the country promoting his book, *Sacredbond: Black Men and Their Mothers*, and seeing its healing power that Keith first suggested I write about my mother and give voice to the stories of women like her, who are so inspirational and often underrepresented.

I want to thank my mother, Pastora Juana Grajales, for teaching me to pursue my dreams and for her prayers and those of the members of her church, Jesus Pacto de Benedicion. A special thanks goes to my sisters: to Luz Thomas for being a good mother and great friend, and to Gladys Perez Johnson for her unending love and below-cost transcription services. Special thanks also to my brothers, Carlos, Alexis, and Joseph.

I want to thank all the "mothers" in my life who shared the same kind of fierce determination in assuring their children's survival, especially my grandmother, the late Cecilia Concepcion, my aunts, the late Ramona Morales, Maria Belen Sanchez and Rosa Sanchez, and the special women who accepted me as a daughter and granddaughter, Constance Brown and Vivian Brown.

Thanks to everyone in my extended family for supporting me in everything I do, especially my father-in-law, Joseph Brown, and brothers-in-law Richard Brown, Mark Thomas, and Anthony Johnson; my nephews, Daniel Thomas and Jacob Thomas; and my nieces, Elise Thomas and Rosalia Perez.

This book could not have been done without the hard work and dedication of the people who contributed to the production of the book, especially Marpessa Dawn Outlaw, Russ Torres, Isabel Rivera, Michele Suite, Sandra Vals, Betel Arnold, and Ana Toro. A very special thank-you goes to Rodney Stringfellow, for helping me realize my vision creatively and logistically and for his dedication to this project from its inception. I could not have done it without you.

I thank HarperCollins and everyone at Rayo, especially my editor, Rene Alegria, for his encouragement and faith in me from our first meeting. I also thank my agents at William Morris, Raul Mateu and Betsy Helf, for always thinking outside the box.

I would also like to thank the following people whose help in putting me in contact with the women of the book was invaluable: Betty de Rio, Kim Flores, Sandra Garcia, Mari Goicolea, Rosalind Rodriguez, Leslie Steele, and Esther Swann.

I want to thank the community of friends and family who helped me realize this vision: Maria Rivera, Sandra Alvarez, Alice Norris, Lisa Jones, Renee Raymond, Linda Carrington, Janice Burgess, Sherrylin Ifill, Gemma Solimene, Rusty O'Kelley; Norma Ortiz and Alena Enid Negron; my West Coast friends Sandra, Janice, Jill, Pam, Loretha, and Cleo, and Fracaswell Hyman—friends who had my back whenever I needed them.

Lastly, I am deeply grateful to Julie Bidwell, whose amazing photographs made this book come alive. Thanks for your vision, patience, and friendship.

—MARIA PEREZ-BROWN
October 2002

TO THE AMAZING Maria Perez-Brown, it's hard to find the words to express how honored I am that you asked me to take the photographs for *Mamá*. It was a great experience from day one, thank you so much! Keith Brown, your friendship is unwavering, thank you for your loyalty and support, always. Rodney Stringfellow and Gladys Perez Johnson, I absolutely could not have done it without you. Thanks to Bobby Holland for your West Coast assistance and to Kim Flores for all of your help in Dallas. Finally, thank you to my son, Brian Bidwell, for never once complaining about my many absences, and to my parents, Jane Bidwell and Bruce Bidwell, and stepmother, Robin Roy, for taking care of him while I was gone.

—JULIE BIDWELL
October 2002

Mamá

Introduction

Maria Perez-Brown

"In search of my mother's garden
I found my own."

—ALICE WALKER

I was five years old when my mother left me. Although I don't remember the exact day or the course of events, I have vivid memories of sitting in a rocking chair on my grandmother's porch in Dorado, Puerto Rico, waving at every airplane that flew over the small oceanfront town. "Is that the plane that Mami took, Abuela?" I would ask my grandmother. And when she answered yes, I would smile and wave even faster. "Adios, Mami. Adios, 747." That, I learned later, was the jet that my mother boarded to come to America.

I asked my mother recently how did a nineteen-year-old girl, not more than a child herself, leave three of her four children with their grandmother and venture to a foreign land where she knew no one and didn't speak the language?

"I had no choice," she answered. My mother was trying to single-handedly change the fate of her three daughters and her handicapped son. She did the only thing she believed would provide her children with a chance for a life beyond the sugarcane fields where we lived. My mother's story is a classic tale of survival, a woman struggling against the odds in order to achieve this purpose. It is a story of a woman who had a dream to make sure that her children's lives would never repeat her own. My mother was relentless in her mission.

Through the anecdotes I heard about my mother from her sisters and cousins, Juana Sanchez Concepcion was an untamable child. She loves to tell vivid, detailed stories about her childhood in Puerto Rico. One of her favorite stories is of how her father used to punish her when she jumped over the fence just to call the lady next door *tuerta*, or "cross-eyed." When asked why she did that despite being told repeatedly not to do so, she says, "Because it was true. She was cross-eyed!" My grandfather, Gregorio Sanchez, was a man of few words. He had little patience left for obstinacy and back talk, especially after he got home from cutting sugarcane all day. Growing up in the Latino culture, you learn early on that respect for your elders is one of our most precious values. Lack thereof would guarantee *una pela*—a good old-fashioned ass whipping. It was that simple.

My grandfather was so strict that he went as far as making my mother drop out of school at the eighth grade because he found a love letter written to her by an admirer, Ramon Perez, the man who eventually became my father. She was fourteen. He was twenty-four. After my grandfather discovered the letters, he gave my mother a whipping from which she still has not recovered. "I sent you to school to learn; not to fall in love," he told her. For eight months my mother was not allowed to leave the front of her house, except when accompanied by one of her parents. But Mami, the untamable one, found a way around that "prison." She and my father would send each other love letters that his little nephew would gladly deliver for five cents. Feeling that there was no reprieve to her "prison" time, Mami agreed to elope with my father.

As Latinas, we are taught that "chastity is a virtue." The belief that women lose their "value" once they are no longer virgins (i.e., nobody would want to marry you) is still pervasive today. For my mother, after the "damage" had been done, my grandparents believed they had no choice but to consent to the union. So my mother and father were married shortly thereafter.

Five years and four children later, Mami found herself alone, struggling to feed her children. My father had immigrated to the United States as a seasonal worker with the promise of sending the money he made back home to feed his children. The money never came. In fact, we did not hear from him for years. With no formal education, Mami took whatever odd job she could to try to make ends meet. Even with the help of her extended family, often there was only white rice and bananas to eat.

Maria Perez-Brown and her mother,
Juana Grajales.

It is hard for me to imagine my mother's life and the struggles she confronted during that time. I now understand that my mother had no choice but to leave her children for a short time in order to provide a better life for them. Those were different times. Puerto Rico in the early sixties was still undergoing a transition from an agricultural society of sugarcane workers to an industrialized society that catered to American industries such as textiles and pharmaceuticals. For Puerto Ricans, like for immigrants all over the world, America held the promise of unlimited opportunities and a way out of poverty. America was believed to be the great equalizer, a land that welcomed people no matter their color or class.

My mother heard that call, and even if it meant leaving her children behind, she was determined to come to America in search of that dream for herself and for her children.

She recently told me that she prepared us for a long time before finally leaving. She said she would sit down with us on the front porch of our one-room wooden house at the edge of the sugarcane field and watch the planes fly by. She would tell us that one day she was going to take a short trip to Nueva York on one of those planes. She told us we were never to cry because she would be gone only a short while, then come back to get us. She told us that if we just smiled and waved she would see us from up in the sky and wave back at us.

I don't recall growing up with a sense of loss or resentment for my mother during the months she was gone. I do remember the joy and excitement I felt when we received the weekly letters and packages Mami would send us. Every week felt like Christmas. Then came the biggest box of all—the one containing matching bright-blue coats with red fur inside. We wore those coats under the hot island sun, just to show our friends that we too would soon be leaving on a 747 jet to join my mother in Nueva York. It had only been three months since Mami left and she kept her promise.

For my mother, America did not necessarily hold up to the promises of a life filled with riches. Like many immigrants who arrive with dreams of making a better life for their families, my mother was forced to work long, hard hours doing menial jobs in factories in order to survive. The poverty we knew in Puerto Rico was replaced by a different kind of urban poverty—one that lacked the freedom of running barefoot outdoors, climbing trees, and playing with other kids in the neighborhood. Because Mami often worked long hours, we were latchkey kids who learned early on to cook, be self-sufficient, and stay locked up inside our apartment until Mami came home. My mother was a strict disciplinarian and we believed that she somehow knew if we had set foot outside when she was not there.

On the occasions that my mother was laid off from her factory jobs we were forced to live off public assistance. During these times we often had to endure humiliation and insults at the hands of the welfare case workers who treated my mom as if she were unemployed by choice. Many times I had to go with my mother to "interpret" for her at the welfare office, although we were just learning to speak English ourselves. But through these difficult times, my mother kept her mission clear—she was going to do what was humanly possible to make sure her children were safe, educated, and successful.

Mamá comes out of a desire to document the stories of remarkable mothers who, like my own, postponed their own dreams and made tremendous sacrifices for their children. I know that every success I've enjoyed in my life comes from my mother's hard work and the strategic decisions she made in our lives. Although sometimes these were drastic decisions—like moving my family to Connecticut when my sister started hanging with the "bad girls" in Brooklyn—they were moves made with the single-minded purpose of improving our lives.

Many of the Latinas you will meet in the following pages feel the same way about their mothers. To many, our mothers are silent, never demanding praise or recognition for all their good deeds. Our mothers' stories are ones of courage. They are stories of great strength, determination, and resilience.

The relationship between Latina mothers and daughters is a complex one. Our mothers are the ones who teach us how to become women. Through their example, they teach us to become loyal wives and mothers, while at the same time teaching us to demand respect and understanding from our husbands. And because of their support, many of us have become successful entrepreneurs and professionals. Our mothers taught us to be strong-willed and independent, while not forgetting the importance of family. But rarely do we get a glimpse of their lives.

In *Mamá* you will meet mothers who continue to defy the odds. It is a testament to everything they helped their daughters with in order to become who they are. Through candid interviews with Latinas across the country, *Mamá* explores the intense bond shared by mothers and daughters. It also explores the generational and cultural differences, the disagreements, the anger, the warmth, the disappointments, the acceptances, and the dreams postponed and encouraged. Through these intimate and intensely personal stories, the daughters talk about how they see themselves reflected in their mothers' eyes as well as how they continue to push barriers to define life in their own terms. *Mamá* explores the lessons daughters have learned from their mothers as well as the legacies they wish they had left behind.

The daughters in *Mamá* are second and third generation Mexicans, Puerto Ricans, Cubans, and Dominicans who were born or grew up in the United States. Some of the women I interviewed are well known—Cristina Saralegui, Celia Cruz, Rosario Dawson, Lauren Velez, Judge Marilyn Milian—and some less known, but all of the women have compelling stories and a unique point of view. The stories they shared cover a spectrum, from the sentiments of love, friendship, pride, and respect to the issues shared by Latinas of race, culture, language, and tradition.

What I learned from the stories is that as Latinas, we have more commonalities than differences. That many of our mothers gave up or postponed dreams of their own to ensure that their daughters had a better life. Most of us experienced some cultural differences between ourselves and our mothers. As Latinas we learned to straddle the two cultures—the cultural values of our mothers and those that we defined for ourselves as modern women living in America. Although these mothers often grew up in a difficult set of circumstances, they were determined to change their children's destinies. In the instances where the mothers did not have a college education, they gave unconditional support and encouragement to their daughters to pursue college careers. And when they did not understand the career choices their daughters made, they supported them anyway, even if that support was little more than a *café con leche* during an all-nighter.

As a daughter of a teen mom, I should have been a statistic. Like my mother, I too should have been a single mother or a high school drop-out living off public assistance. But this was unacceptable to my mother. Instead, I became a Yale University graduate, who became a lawyer who owns her own television production company. Instead, I inherited my mother's spirit of rebel-lion and determination. I inherited my mother's vision and sense of adventure. The untamable one instilled in my sisters and me that we did not have to fulfill the prophecy that was expected of three Puerto Rican girls growing up without a father. My

mother gave me a legacy that as a Latina I had the ability to struggle against the odds and win. If my mother could accomplish what she did at nineteen with four children, I had no choice but to succeed at the most insurmountable task before me. I had no choice but to become a woman who reflects most of what my mother values and everything that she struggled for and fought against. I had no choice but to validate her life through my own. ■

A Sacrifice for the Quinceañera

Rosario Marin

AND HER MOTHER,

Carmen Spindola

One of six children born to a housewife and a factory worker in Mexico City, Rosario Marin rose to become the first Mexican-born U.S. treasurer. As in a classic immigrant story, Rosario went from being a girl "with one pair of good shoes" to being the highest-ranking Latina to serve in President George W. Bush's administration. ■ Although Rosario's political career, which included being mayor and councilwoman of Huntington Park, California, has taken her far from the very traditional world of her mother, Carmen, both women find that it is their families that inspire them to continue to push forward.

WHEN ROSARIO MARIN was fourteen years old her mother, Carmen, told her that their family would be moving from Mexico to live in the United States. But Rosario, at the time, the second-oldest of five brothers and sisters, did not want to go. "I cried and cried," Rosario recalls. "I really did not want to leave because of *mis quince años*." Rosario was about to turn fifteen and her *Quinceañera* was only months away. Rosario had fantasies of what she wanted her *Quinceañera* to be. Most important, she wanted to celebrate her *Quinceañera* with the friends she had known since childhood. The last thing she wanted was to celebrate such an important occasion in a foreign country, with people she didn't know. She was not about to give in. Not understanding that her family was poor, Rosario insisted on having her *Quinceañera* where she wanted it. Her mother made a deal with her.

"My mother promised me that we would go back home to Mexico six months later and celebrate my birthday with the friends I'd left behind," Rosario says. That promise was enough to convince Rosario to make the trip with her mother, father, and two of her four siblings.

"My two little brothers stayed back home. The embassy denied the visas to all of us together because there were too many of us," Rosario sadly recalls. "They felt that my dad couldn't afford to feed, clothe, and house us all, so they separated us. But eventually the boys came along. My baby sister, Nancy, was born here in the United States.

"I never really knew I was poor because I was so rich in having my mom prepare food for us and take care of us.

When I was in elementary school, every day around ten-thirty in the morning, my mother would bring *café con leche, un pan, y una torta* to us at school. Sometimes we only had one pair of shoes, that was the good pair, and then we had the *chanclas* (sandals), which we used the rest of the time. By the end of the school year you didn't know which one was the good pair of shoes. But I had a very enriching childhood.

"A couple of years after my youngest sister was born, I was already in high school. My dad would work at night so that he could stay at home to take care of the baby. My mom would work during the day, then she would come back home and my dad would go to work. It was pretty hectic. When I finished high school, it was my duty to work full-time so that my mom could stay home and take care of the baby. It's interesting that my brother was allowed to go to school during the day 'because the man needs to have a higher education.' He was going to be a provider, while I was going to be a 'providee.' In the eyes of my parents, finishing high school was the biggest accomplishment expected of a girl.

"But finishing high school was far more than they could have done had we stayed in Mexico. So when my brother and I finished high school at the same time, they said, 'Okay, my job is done. I'm very proud my children finished high school and that's it.' But my brother and I both wanted to go to college. My parents decided that my brother could go to school full-time and work part-time and I would go to work full-time. I decided to go to school part-time, anyway.

"At that time, it was what the family said that ruled and we all had to agree. I could not question why my brother got to go to school and not me. This was twenty-five years ago. It was not seen as denying me an opportunity, it was just the way things were and it was okay. I had no problem going to work so that my mom could stay home and take care of my sister, because at the time I believed that I was going to get married and someone was going to provide for me.

"I went to East L.A. College at night and began to work in a factory during the day. I started as a shipping clerk and eventually was promoted to customer service. My mom would say something like, '¿Ay mi'ja, pero si ya eres secretaria, para que tienes que ir a la escuela?' [You're a secretary already, why do you have to go to school?] My mother wondered why I sacrificed myself to go to school at night when I wasn't working on the factory floor anymore; I was working in the office!

"Most days I would come home at ten or at ten-thirty at night. I remember driving to my little house and my mom would be waiting for me by the window, wondering what time I was going to come home. I would say, 'Mom, but I need to do this. I need to finish college.' When I finished at East L.A. College, my mom was very impressed. It took me four years to get my two-year degree, but she was very happy that I finally got my college education. She thought I was done, but at that time I realized that it was not enough; if I wanted to get ahead, I had to get my bachelor's degree. So I enrolled in Cal State Los Angeles. My mom said, 'Pero mi'ja, but you already

graduated from college.' I'd say, 'Yeah, Mom, but I have to go!'

"Sometimes when I had to do term papers at night, until three o'clock or four o'clock, my mother would be sitting right next to me. What is really amazing is that even though she couldn't understand why I had to go to school and though she couldn't help me (she couldn't type and she certainly didn't know anything about English or chemistry), she was sitting right there by my side, feeding me and giving me café con leche." Rosario laughs and says, "Maybe that's why she didn't want me to go to school anymore, because she wanted to go to sleep!"

Rosario's mother saw the sacrifices that Rosario was making in order to pursue her education and she became concerned that it was taking a toll on her daughter. "Only as time goes by can I appreciate it, because this was a woman who did the only thing she could do—sit by me."

Rosario eventually graduated with a business degree from Cal State Los Angeles and went on to build an impressive career in banking. She was on the corporate fast track and about to be named Vice President for City National Bank when her first son, Eric, was born. "My first child, Eric, was born with Down syndrome. Obviously, it was devastating for me. It was the most tragic event in my life. I said, 'God, why are you punishing

me? I've been a good daughter. I am certainly a good wife. I've been a good sister. I've been a good neighbor. I've been a good worker. Why are you punishing me this way to give me this child?' I remember the night I was giving birth to Eric, I was taken to the hospital to have an emergency C-section. My mom came to visit my newborn son and me.

"I was just yelling and screaming, and I was in deep, tremendous pain. My mom said, 'Ay, mi'ja, stop crying. It hurts me a lot to see you like this.' And I said, 'Oh, Mom, you don't understand,' and she says, 'I do. I do understand. I have six children.' And I said, 'Yes, but none of them are retarded.' I remember saying it and feeling really guilty about it. My mom said, 'You know, mi'ja, you are right; you hurt for one but I hurt for two. I hurt for him and for you.'

"I stayed home after Eric was born. I gave up my entire career. I was going to be named assistant vice president for the bank that I worked for. I had started working towards my MBA and we had a beautiful house. But all of that went down the toilet because I had to stop working. That expectation came from the Mexican side of my family. Again, there was no question—that was just the way it was supposed to be. By that time I had already done so much with my life, and it ruined my career. I didn't have a job; I had a career. I had

already planned what I was going to do with the next thirty years of my life."

The struggle of coping with Eric's disability propelled Rosario into politics, first as an advocate for children with disabilities then as a two-time councilwoman of Huntington Park. Rosario gives full credit to her mother for helping her with Eric during this time.

"My mother really helped me out with Eric. She took care of Eric while I went back to work. My mother has eighteen grandchildren now, but her favorite is Eric and that's just a very special gift. The first five years of Eric's life, there were about six occasions where we thought Eric was going to die. At first you pray for a specific outcome. I did. I prayed to God with all my heart that Eric would be cured. Obviously that didn't happen. Then my mom would say, 'Just pray that we are able to accept the will of God. Pray for acceptance and faith that the will of God prevails and that if you allow it, it will be for your benefit.' So I stopped praying for specific outcomes; now I only pray for wisdom, tolerance, strength, and courage to face whatever it is that I'm going to be facing.

"I've always said that my mother is

a saint, a woman of incredible faith. She's always been a role model as a mother and a grandmother. My hope is that I can emulate those qualities.

"When I was told that President Bush was going to appoint me as treasurer of the United States, I had to let my mother know ahead of time because she has heart problems and I didn't want her to be completely blindsided and get very emotional. She had known that I was being considered for something, but I was prohibited from telling anybody what it was. Once it happened, and I knew the president was going to make the announcement, I sat her down and I said, 'Mom, you know that I am being considered for a position. I want you to know that the president is going to say that he wants me to be the next treasurer of the United States.' I could see my mom was having one of these *mareos* [dizzy spells]. Then she got quiet and said, '*¿Ay mi'ja, que no es eso mucha responsabilidad?*' [Isn't that a lot of responsibility?] And I said, '*Sí*, Mom.' Then she said, '*¿Porqué no te podrían dar algo mas abajito?*' She wanted to know if they could give me something a little bit lower! Here I was about to be the treasurer of the United States and my mom is worried about her little girl. I said, 'Mom, the president thinks that I can do it.' She finally understood '*Ay, mi'ja*, well, if this is going to be good for you . . .'

"I'm very lucky. I have the best mom in the world. I have always told my mother how much I love her. On my birthday, I have always sent her flowers, ever since I was nineteen years of age. It was interesting because the first time she got the flowers she thought that somebody had sent them to her because they had accidentally written 'Carmen' on the card.

"So when the governor appointed me to this big position, she was there by my side. When they gave me an award at the United Nations, she was there by my side. And for my swearing in as the treasurer of the United States, she was right there, front row. She deserves that. When I got married, I said, 'I want everybody to know that if I have a daughter my mother's name is going to be hers—that's taken, don't anybody else take it.' I always say that the two most important women in my life are named Carmen—my daughter and my mother. Carmen means song, so I'm always with music.

"I would do anything for my mom; she's a great gift. Now I realize the incredible sacrifice that she had to make so that I could have my *Quinceañera*. Six months after arriving in the United States my mother took me back to Mexico for my party. She kept her promise. It's amazing. I remember the dress she bought me; for her it was a big deal. It wasn't really the most beautiful dress but to me it was. My mom had sparkles in her eyes looking for that little dress. I look at it now and it's a very simple dress—it was long with little rhinestones. She made my bouquet out of plastic flowers, and to me it was the most beautiful *ramo* that I could find. She cut one of the paper napkins with that lacey look that come under cakes and put it behind the plastic flowers. When I got married, my bouquet cost a hundred and fifty dollars. The *Quinceañera* was in the patio of our house. To me it was the happiest day of my life. Today I could buy things that are so expensive, but the things that move me the most are the things that have no price that my mommy has given me." ∎

The Twenty-Four-Hour Women

Maria Hinojosa

AND HER MOTHER,

Berta Hinojosa

Maria Hinojosa is an award-winning correspondent for CNN and the anchor of *Latino USA*, a weekly national radio program on NPR. *Hispanic Business* magazine twice named Maria one of the 100 Most Influential Latinos in the United States. Maria is the author of the acclaimed memoir *Raising Raul: Adventures Raising Myself and My Son* and *Crews: Gang Members Talk to Maria Hinojosa*. ■ Berta Hinojosa is no less busy or driven than her prominent daughter. Born and raised in Mexico City, Berta immigrated to Chicago, Illinois, where she developed and was named director of the domestic violence and sexual assault programs at Mujeres Latinas en Acción. Berta is a nationally recognized leader and spokeswoman for Latina abuse victims. Recognized as a Hispanic Woman of the Year by the city of Chicago, she and her daughter have learned together how to make a difference in their worlds as well as in their families.

THE TWENTY-FOUR-HOUR WOMEN

MARIA HINOJOSA remembers a pivotal moment that forever affected the way she would look at having both a career and a family. Her mother, Berta, had just announced that she wanted to work outside of the home. This was not a casual statement—it was a bold declaration of independence. And as with most declarations of independence, it was followed by a civil war.

The day that Berta made her declaration, there was a heated argument and then twelve-year-old Maria watched as her father resisted and told his wife that he did not want her to work. "My father was saying, 'No. This is not what I want to have in a wife,'" Maria recalls. "My mother said, 'This is who I am.' I guess that that's been one of the most central forming moments in my life as a working woman.

"Seeing that issue played out so clearly in my own household made me realize how much that moment in my mother's life meant," recalls Maria, "and how much determination she had for wanting to work." Although Maria and her siblings supported their mother's right to go to work one hundred percent, they did not want their parents to get divorced over this issue. "I did not support having a divorced household. That I wasn't going to have. I remember putting my foot down and saying, 'If you get a divorce, I'll kill myself!'

"I think that was essentially the wake-up call for my father. He needed to realize that I was gonna support my mom. The whole family understood that this was important for my mother because we were all growing up in this country during the feminist movement— we were living it. This was the early 1970s and we were American kids watching this and experiencing this in Chicago."

The youngest of four children, Maria was born in Mexico, where her parents lived. "My mom essentially left school to marry my father, but my father was studying to become a doctor, so that was fine," explains Maria. "In the sense of what was valued there, they knew that my mother was going to be provided for. She was marrying a man who was going to provide for her. So her role was to be *una buena mamá* [a good mother] and a good wife."

The Hinojosa family was forced to change their plans when the Mexican government changed. As the old administration stepped down, so did many of its plans, including the planned construction of a hospital that was supposed to employ Maria's father. "Suddenly the position that my father thought he was going to have in this hospital went away because the government changed. And there he was with four kids and no job. So when he got a job offer in Chicago, we had to go."

Leaving her home in Mexico, Berta packed her four kids and boarded a plane to Chicago, where she would join her husband. The next eight years of her life would be a crash course in learning a new language and a new culture.

"We were in a neighborhood where there were many women who were academics, many women who were not just housewives. They were our neighbors and my mom met and talked to them. I think this inspired her. My mom decided that she wanted to do something other than perfect the art of making a bed or ironing sheets. The first thing she did was tell my father she wanted to volunteer at the hospital where he worked, helping the Spanish-speaking patients. That is how it started for her.

"My mom really got into her work. At first she was volunteering just one afternoon a week, then she was volunteering two afternoons, three afternoons, four afternoons, five afternoons, then all of a sudden she was named volunteer of the year. The rumblings were heard loudly throughout my house. My father said, 'What's going on? Enough of this volunteer stuff, enough of you doing what you think you have to do!' And all the kids are watching this; we're all just studying it.

"Then something happened that created a financial need. One of my siblings wasn't doing so well in school, and it was recommended that he should go to a private school. My parents say, 'Okay, but there's no money.' That's when one of my mom's friends told her about a store that was looking for someone to help sell clothing. And so my mom told my dad that she wanted to start working. Over the span of a year, there was a tremendous amount of tension, discussion, anger, and accusations. It was the most dramatic, emotional, and divisive period in my family. My father totally felt like he was losing the woman that he had married. He said, 'You are not the woman who I married. I did not marry a woman who wanted to go to work every day. I married Berta Ojeda. This was not part of the deal.' And my mom struggled to say, 'But this is who I am. Look at where we're living now. This is the new life that we have; we're not in Mexico, we're in Chicago. There are women who are doing things here.' She just kept on going and I think that my father realized that it could become a breaking point, that it was about more than just bringing in a couple extra dollars to the home for my mother. It was about my mother finding herself."

Berta took the job as a saleswoman at the clothing store that catered to the professional women of the city. "My mom would spend her days figuring out how these women needed to look in their jobs, whether they were lawyers, accountants, or whatever. I think that my mom thought, 'Wait a second. I don't have to just dress them; I could be like them. Being a mom and a wife was something that brought her extraordinary satisfaction, but she knew that there was something else she could be. This was in the late sixties, early seventies, and she saw younger women doing it and she said, 'Me too.' "

Berta put in eight to ten years at the clothing store. After Maria left for college, Berta took a position as a social worker at an organization called Mujeres Latinas en Acción. In a short while, she became one of the top Latina social workers in the city of

Berta Hinojosa and her daughter,
Maria Hinojosa, in New York City.

Chicago, specifically geared toward Latina victims of domestic abuse. Maria proudly says, "Then she was on the governor's commission and on the mayor's commission. She was getting named this and that by the city and by the state and she started attending national conferences. There was nothing that could stop her. It wasn't a verbal thing like, 'Mira mi'jita, look at all the walls I'm breaking down and look at what I'm doing,' it was just her focus."

That focus and responsibility is also reflected in Berta's daughter. "I think that there's a mission in my life. As a journalist, I always knew that my mission was to give visibility to those who are invisible. I understood very clearly that my father had a mission in his work as a medical doctor, he studied deafness as a mission. I think for my mom, her first mission was to have an identity other than a mom. Then her mission became working with these women who really were the disadvantaged and the abused. We all have missions."

Contemporary Latinas, having lived through the rise of feminism and having grasped the brass rings in their careers, still find themselves trying to live up to an idealistic and sometimes unrealistic portrayal of what a Latina mother should be. When Maria decided to start a family of her own, it was difficult to find a role model for what type of mother she would be. "For me all the women in my extended family were exemplary mothers, who would sacrifice everything for their kids. I grew up seeing that the ideal Latina mother is a woman who gives up herself for her kids, the mother is always thinking about her children, what is she gonna do for her children? What is best for her children? It is a woman who has total devotion, not only to the children but also to the family and the husband. That's why when I thought about becoming a mother, I thought that is not who I am."

Maria feels that as Latinas, we have to break out of that illusion because not all Latina mothers are like that. As women living in America our realities have changed and we have many more factors to consider in addition to being good mothers. In determining what kind of mother she would be, Maria says she had to ask herself many questions. "I was also raised in this country where you are taught to think about yourself and your career goals, about putting yourself forward, about what do you want? What's your goal? That's why it was very hard to conceive that I could be that Latina mother ideal."

Unlike her mother, Maria found herself among the first generation of women who grew up with a choice. She was among the beneficiaries of earlier generations of women who struggled to get equal rights and equal income. For her it was a given that women could have the same career choices as men. The notion that these liberated young women would have to compromise their professional aspirations to become mothers never occurred to them. But the idea of compromise came from an unexpected place, it came from their own ideas of what motherhood was, what it should be, and, significantly, what it could be. To try to achieve the ideal of the sacrificing Latina mother was an elusive goal. More and more, it seems that the rules for motherhood have irreversibly changed.

Maria had to confront the dilemma that young Latinas trying to raise a family often have to confront—"How do we raise our children to have the same values that my parents had fifty years ago? It's a very elusive dance. How much do you keep? How much don't you keep? It's very different than how my mom was being raised and how my mom raised us."

One of the things that Maria has held on to is the physical affection she learned to receive from her mother. Although her days were filled with taking care of the needs of four children, Berta always had time to give affection to her kids. "There's a photo that I have of me and my mom in which my mom is riding a two-wheel bike and she has me on the little chair in the back. That was Mami and daughter time, me being with her. Being the youngest, I accompanied my mom everywhere if she was cleaning the house or wherever she needed to go. I always felt secure with my mom being in the same place that I was. Maybe she wasn't playing dolls with me, but just knowing that she was near gave me this instant sense of peace. And I think about that in terms of my own daughter. I think when I'm there, that there's a sense of calm for her. Maybe I'm not right there, playing with her, but she knows that I'm there if she needs me. She can run up to me and say, 'Mamá.' Or she does what I did with my mom, I would just run up to her wherever she was and just wrap my arms around her and hug her. She would always give me a hug back, *o sobarme la espalda o los brasitos* [or rub my back or my arms]. That physical aspect is something that I feel is very much a part of who I am and one of the things that I feel strongly about handing down to my children."

One of the things that was very hard for Maria was when she realized that the traditional roles were reversed in her family, with her husband being the one who would stay at home.

"Suddenly, I felt like I wasn't gonna be that mom that stays at home with her children; I was the one who was gonna be like my father. I was the one who would leave the house every day and then say hello to the kids at the end of the day, the way my father did. I felt very self-critical. Of course, I know there was some rumbling from my family in Mexico—'What do you mean she works and he stays at home?' Even though he is an artist and he's working at home, I think they have a real hard time understanding that a man could want to be with his children or feel that that is important. I remember early on feeling like this is a whole other level of breaking molds that I have no role model for at all."

When reflecting on whether she could be a stay-at-home mom like her mother was, Maria says, "There are some times when I'll see my children doing something and I say to myself, 'If I were staying home, that wouldn't be happening. There wouldn't be a temper tantrum or they wouldn't do this.' Sometimes I feel guilty because I've seen so many people wish that they could be with their children more."

What makes this dilemma even more complicated for Maria and women like her is that oftentimes they are "the first" at whatever they are doing and they feel the responsibility of being a role model to other Latinas. "Because as a Latina who's trying to go where Latinas haven't gone before, you have the weight of history and of your community on your back, I don't feel that I can say, 'Okay, good-bye, I'm leaving my job and I'm gonna be a full-time mom.' What about all of those young people who have thought of me and said, 'Wow, she opened doors, she was a professional, she was the first Latina at CNN and NPR and now she's just gonna give it all up?' I have a responsibility. As a journalist, what do I want to leave as a legacy? What doors do I want to open, understanding the importance of that legacy? On the other hand, when I look at my children I say, 'My God, they are my legacy and they came out of me. They have to be the best reflection of who I am and my values. But how do I give that to them if I'm working all the time?' "

Like many women, Maria has to balance being a professional with being a responsible mother. She has to balance being an American with being a Mexican-American. The conflict of interests sometimes can be enormous. Maria tends to believe the struggle comes with the territory. "I don't think that there's resolution. I've always felt very discombobulated because I have these two parts of myself, my Latina self and my gringa self. I remember I had just gotten to New York, I was eighteen years old, and I bought a little pin that said *soy bilingue, bicultural, y orgullosa de mi raza* [I am bilingual, bicultural, and proud of my race]. And I put it on and I said, 'Damn, I'm gonna be bilingual and bicultural for the rest of my life. This is how it's gonna be forever.' You're always gonna be discombobulated because you're a bi."

Despite all of the heavy baggage Maria has to contend with, or perhaps because of it, she has carved out an

ambitious and groundbreaking career as well as establishing a happy and loving home for her family. When she looks back on the very traditional upbringing she had, she admits that her parents always wanted her to further herself. And that always included college and a career.

"My mom and dad never sat down with me and said, 'Maria, you can be whatever you want to be.' It was unspoken. I understood that I was definitely going to go to college and that I was going to probably have a career, but from there the ending part of it gets a little fuzzy."

Maria says, however, that her mother had her own set of expectations for her youngest daughter. When it came to making alternative choices, her mother was her greatest supporter. "My mother has lived vicariously through me," explains Maria. "I was the one who was able to do all the things that she wasn't able to do. When I came home one day and I said, 'You know, I want to go to New York for college.' My dad was like, 'What?' And my mom was like, 'What?' But then she said, 'Okay.' She was my greatest backer, but I always wonder whether or not I'm living up to her expectations as a mother. She would probably say that I have, but for me I don't think I've met that challenge. For me, my mother is the best possible mom."

Maria says wistfully, "Sometimes I wish my mom was more of the kind of grandmother to my children that my *abuelita* was to me. My *abuelita* was the kind of grandmother that would come and take care of me. She would clean and sew my clothes at night and cook all these things for me. When my mom became a working woman she did those things less than my grandmother did. Now my mom is a young retiree and she's traveling a lot. My parents have a home in Mexico, so she's doing her thing.

"I've said to her, 'I kind of wish you would be less of a hip, fabulous, feminist, young retiree and more of an *abuelita* to my kids. I wish she would be more like a, 'What do you need, *mi'jitos,* I'll be there for you' type of grandmother. But that's where I have to let go of my own preconceptions of what

she should be. I have a lot of letting go to do.

"The thing about my mom and I is that we're very aware of these dichotomies in our lives," says Maria. "We know that there are taboo things that we are not supposed to talk about as Latinas, but then there's a part of us that is like modern gringas and that we think we're supposed to be able to talk about them. I remember when I said to my mom, 'Mom, you never talked to me about sex.' She told me, '*¿Como que no? Pero yo siempre les he comunicado que el sexo es una cosa linda y preciosa y que es algo muy especial entre dos gente que se quieren.*' [What do you mean? I have always told you that sex is a beautiful and special thing between two people who love each other.] I said, 'You never said that to me.' There was a lot of stuff around the whole sex thing that we never communicated on.

"Now my mom and I try to talk about things that we're not supposed to talk about. I think that we've become more modern. And when it gets really funky and there's stuff between us that gets really intense and heavy and problematic, we see a shrink together. We have a therapist who happens to be a Puerto Rican sister from the Bronx who is just wonderful and who is a friend to the both of us. So in those moments when it's gotten really hard, we've gone to see her. I know there are some people in my family who probably say, 'You're doing *what* with your mama? Going to see a therapist?!'

"My mom was actually the first one in the family to do therapy. She needed to deal with the death of her father and with the whole craziness in the household over her working. So she opened that door. Again, something that none of her sisters or cousins or anybody in Mexico would have done. In that sense she'll do what she feels she needs to do."

The latest thing Berta has needed to do is take up scuba diving. With a broad smile, Maria explains, "She learned at sixty years old, both her and my father. My mom didn't even know how to swim and she learned how to scuba dive. She has an adventurous spirit that was handed down to her from my grandmother. In Mexico, they used to say that my grandmother *'tenia pata de perro,'* which means you were always going out on an adventure. And that's my mom as well.

"She just amazes me. She amazes me with her spirit and her determination and the fact that she'll go out and learn how to scuba dive and she'll go on an African safari and she'll do all these things she's never done before. She'll open up the doors for my father to think, 'Yeah, let's do this.' She's just unstoppable." ∎

Chica, Interrupted

Jackie Guerra

AND HER MOTHER,

Joyce Guerra

Jackie Guerra is an actress making a lot of noise in Hollywood. Currently Jackie is the host of *You're Invited* on the Style Network and is featured in the highly acclaimed PBS series *American Family.* Jackie starred in the WB series *First Time Out* and made her film debut in the Warner Bros. movie *Selena.* Prior to her acting career, Jackie worked as an organizer with the Democratic Party and HERE, Local 11, and worked closely with Cesar Chavez in support of his farmworker's union. ■ Jackie learned both her activism and her outrageousness from her mother, Joyce Guerra. Through the force of her will, Joyce was able to take her painful childhood and transform it into an incredible and rich life. She has passed her refusal to be defined by her circumstances on to her daughter, who creates new worlds of her own while dealing with the unexpected death of her mother.

CHICA, INTERRUPTED

JACKIE GUERRA'S MOTHER once told her, "Give me the flowers when I'm alive. I don't want people wasting money and picking beautiful flowers out of the earth to put on a big, brown box that's going to be in the ground. I don't want my body underground decaying. I'd rather be thin in life." Little did Jackie know that she would be thinking about these words as she was making preparations to have her mother's body cremated and the ashes scattered off the coast of San Diego. Her mother's sudden and unexpected death happened just two and a half weeks from what would have been her fifty-seventh birthday. Up to then, Jackie had been having the best year of her life.

"I was about to do a talk show pilot, and it was a time in my life where everything was going great. The movie *Selena* had just come out and I had offers to do all these other movies. I had a deal with Dick Clark at Disney to do a talk show that I was going to host, which has always been my dream."

Jackie's life suddenly became busier than it ever had been, as she began work on her talk show pilot while continuing to do her stand-up comedy routine. At the same time, she continued to keep up with her family and friends. On July 4, one of her best friends, Beth, had her first child, so Jackie and her mother decided to surprise her by filling her freezer with prepared food so that she wouldn't have to cook—a gesture that was typical of Joyce's thoughtfulness and generosity.

"That afternoon we were going to go to the mall and then we were going to go home and cook. My mother called and said she didn't want to go to the mall, which is like really out of character for her. I mean my mother was a shopper!

"We went to my house and I was in the kitchen doing something and I looked in the living room and she was lying on my couch. I'd never seen her lay down in the middle of the afternoon, ever. She was like superwoman. My mom was the kind of person that never ever complained—the exact opposite of me. In fact, one time she had a fractured ankle and she walked around with it for three weeks before she ever said anything about it."

When Joyce told her daughter she didn't feel well, Jackie took her to the hospital, where she was admitted. While she got progressively worse, the doctors couldn't figure out what was wrong. Jackie continued to tell herself that everything had to be okay.

"My mom and I would talk every day. There are times even now when I'll see something and say, 'I can't wait to tell the Crayon.'" Jackie called her mother "the Crayon" because she would always dress in one color from head to toe. "So if it was a red day, it was red lipstick, and an outfit in different shades of red, red shoes, and red nail polish. Her nails were always done. No matter what was going on in my mother's life, she always had her nails done; the perfect manicure and the perfect pedicure. And she always had the hair and the makeup done. My mom wore false eyelashes ever since I could remember. Literally her last day on this earth, she had perfect eyelashes."

Being the daughter of such an attractive and flamboyant woman made Jackie compare herself unfavorably to her mother. "I always felt like I was very ugly and she was very pretty. The women in my family are very beautiful and I always felt like I was the ugly one. My mom used to say to me, 'Do you think that Jacqueline Kennedy walked around thinking that she was too skinny? No. She just bought clothes that were one size bigger so that people would think she was chic and thin.' My mother used to always tell me that I should act like Elvis (because she was real big with these American icons). She would say, 'You know Elvis Presley is the biggest star that the world has ever known. And people will climb over each other just for the opportunity to maybe get a piece of Elvis's sweat on them. You walk in the room like you are Elvis. You walk in that room and you are the biggest star in the world. People are so lucky that they are in the room that you are walking into.'

"I never thought of weight as an issue until I got older. It wasn't until I was in high school and would wear shorts to school and the white girls in my school would make comments about me having thunder thighs. I would go home and tell my mother and she would say, 'Oh, they are jealous of you.' That's when I started to understand that there's a whole culture out there that said you were supposed to be skinny and have straight hair. And if you could be blonde, then you really won the genetic lottery. But to my mom, I could weigh 130 pounds or 230 pounds, I was still the most amazing, the most special, the most interesting, charming, charismatic person on earth. The good news is that I didn't have a lot of issues that young girls have, the bad news is when mom's not there anymore I don't have that voice anymore."

A few days after the visit to the hospital, Jackie and her mother went to the beauty supply store and Jackie noticed that she was groggy and couldn't shop. Jackie had to put her in the car and take her home. The family continued to ask the doctor what was wrong, but they were given no answer. "We knew she was sick, but we thought she had the flu. But she just kept getting worse. We didn't know she was dying."

One morning Jackie came to visit her mother and found her passed out on the floor. She was able to wake her up but Joyce couldn't move. "My mom was tiny, but lifting her that day was lifting dead weight. So I called my fiancé and he came and we got her back in the bed. We know now that she had a stroke, but nobody had diagnosed it then."

Joyce was born in Colorado and left home at an early age. She went to Chicago, got a fake ID, and worked as a bunny at a Playboy club. "At that point, she was fifteen and she was a hottie. My mom had a brutal life as a child. The oldest of six kids, she had a terrible home life, and was the victim of sexual abuse as a child.

"My mother was beyond poor. The first time she ever took us to see where she grew up, we were shocked. I mean there is poor and then there is the kind of poor you don't see. It's the kind of poor that documentaries get made about. That's how she grew up. They didn't have a bathroom in their house. They grew up in the snow and they had one pair of shoes. This is not one of those stories people make up. I mean they literally had one pair of shoes."

Jackie's mother was haunted by her childhood. Jackie recalls, "My mother told me that the best thing she could do for herself was to create a whole new life because she never wanted her kids or anybody else to go through what she went through."

Joyce was married for a brief period while in Chicago. She later left for California, working as a cocktail waitress outside of San Diego, where the man who would become Jackie's father was the restaurant's dishwasher. "My dad had just come to the United States and didn't speak any English. Of course, my mom spoke perfect English. My dad is really good-looking and my mom was nearly single and thinking she was so cool because she had a brand-new convertible that her first husband had bought her. She didn't have money to pay for her rent, but she had a brand-new convertible Corvette. She actually asked my dad out. And my dad said, 'Mira, esta mujer.' My dad thought that she was one of those forward American women and he was not going to go out with her."

But Joyce would not be deterred and they eventually fell in love and moved in together. "Nobody was doing that in 1965. Even though she pretended to be the perfect suburban housewife, my parents lived together for two years until her divorce was final and that was super scandalous in my dad's family. First of all, that he was marrying an American, because if you are born here, the Mexicans of Mexico consider you American. The fact that he was with an American and she was older and she was divorced was scandalous." Joyce's mother-in-law barely spoke to her for the first two years of their marriage. It wasn't until Jackie was born that she started being nice to her.

"My mom was always very creative. At Christmastime, she made her own wrapping paper. I honestly don't know how she did it. I really wish my mother were here just to admit to me that she was on something because I don't understand how she did what she did. Every morning we got up she had already made breakfast and was dressed for her day. Every day she took us to school. Every night there was dinner. Every night. And she worked. She sold real estate. She was always saleswoman of the year, selling a million dollars worth of real estate.

"I think that the good news is that my mom had so much energy and was always on the go, but the bad news is that she forgot to put herself first. My brother and I were incredibly spoiled." When Jackie moved into her first apartment during her freshman year of college, she realized that she didn't know how to run a dishwasher, or a washing machine, or a vacuum cleaner. "My brother and I are named after the Kennedys. I'm Jackie and he's John. That says so much about my mother. From the time I was very little, she always took great pride in things that aren't typical.

"My mom had this thing that anything you want to do, you can do. Whether you are the best or not, just try it. Try everything. I do think that there is something in teaching children they can do anything. If I came home and said I wanted to learn to play guitar, the next day I had guitar lessons. If I said I think I'd like to paint, I was in painting classes. The thing that happens is that you sort of become jack-of-all-trades and master of none. So I can do a lot of things a little bit, but there is no one thing that I'm great at. Except I'm very fun at parties.

"My mother really understood that this is a big world and that we are citizens of a big world and I think that's because she did come from such a small place in such a hideous world where she could've easily been trapped. She escaped by learning about the world."

Jackie's mother insisted that her daughter learn about the world as well by going to college. After she graduated, her mother was less than happy that Jackie began working for a nonprofit center that paid her next to no money. "My mother said, 'You should go to law school so you can help these people by being a lawyer.' Because for Latinas, it's all about the title and you have to be the lawyer or engineer.

"My parents worked hard so that we could have security. In her mind being successful meant never having to depend on anybody else economically. So when I told them I was working as a labor union organizer my mom was worried because I was working literally eighteen hours a day and I never had a day off. I was young, I didn't have a boyfriend and I had no life. When she was my age, there were five different guys begging her to marry them and she was collecting engagement rings. So to her it was like, 'How can you be my daughter?'

"One day my mom shows up at my house with all this stuff like shoes and for no apparent reason, this very sexy underwear. I said '¿Y eso?' and she said, 'You never know.' And I'm like, 'Okay, whatever. This is so uncomfortable.' My mom and I were in the kitchen, just chitchatting, and all of a sudden, like a total telenovela, she drops the spatula and looks at me. She goes, 'Are you a *lesbiana?*' And I'm like, 'What? Where did this come from?' And she goes, 'I don't know. I don't see men calling you. I've been here for two

Jackie Guerra on the beach in Santa Monica, California.

days and no one has called. I hear the voices in the machine and I don't hear men.' I told her, 'Rest assured I'm not a lesbian, if I were I would tell you.' And she said, 'I will love you. I will love you, I promise.' All I could tell her was 'Thank you, but you can put the I love my gay daughter T-shirt away for now.' "

As their relationship changed, Joyce felt that she could share more of herself with her daughter. So she was excited to tell Jackie that, after all those years, she had enrolled in college to take an erotic writing course. "She said it's just an exploration of women and sexuality and I thought, 'Oh, that's interesting. That's kind of cool.' Until the point where she decided that it's okay to call me at seven in the morning on a Sunday to read me an essay that she's written for her class. It was entitled 'The Exploration of the Orgasm.' And then she used the word 'fuck' as a verb. I said, 'Mom, just so you know, I'm very happy for you and I really encourage you to take college courses, but at the same time the only time I ever want to hear the word f-u-c-k out of your mouth is if you stub your toe or someone drops something on your foot. Never as a verb. Never ever as a verb.' It was so horrible. I guess she felt I got to an age where she could loosen up and tell me things. But I was like, 'Oh, my God; I liked it better when I wasn't allowed to curse in front of you.'

"One time I remember she was at my house and I had to take a shower. So she's sitting in my room talking to me but I'm in the shower and the bathroom door is open. I get out of the shower and I kind of shut the door a little bit because I was standing there naked. And she stands up, opens the door, and goes, 'If you are not comfortable being naked in front of your mother, how are you going to be comfortable being naked in front of a man?' And she's like men love it if you just walk around comfortably in front of them. I told her, 'Mother, I really didn't need to know that.' "

Just as Jackie got to watch her relationship with her mother grow and change, she also got the opportunity to share her good fortune with her mother. "One time, my mother and I went to Chicago and we stayed in the most beautiful hotel. It's right on the lake and we stayed in this suite and it was like twenty-five hundred dollars a night. My mom loved it. We called down and had somebody come up to give her a manicure in the room. And she got the fluffy robe from the hotel and really thought she was a big baller living large. And when my show, *First Time Out*, got canceled, which was like a month after we had done this trip, I was so upset because I felt like we just wasted that money. I thought, 'I'll never work again and I'll be selling shoes at Nordstrom's tomorrow.' I was so upset about the money.

"But I couldn't have known that my mother was going to be dead in a year and when she died I was so grateful to God that I had taken her to Chicago and spent that money because what would I have saved it for? What would I have spent it on when she was gone? It was so much fun to see her face at the airport when they said we are now boarding our first class passengers and she was like, 'That's us, *mi'ja*. Let's go.' In Las Vegas there was a leather store and they had a leather jacket that had a leather rainbow on the back. My mother put it on and it was just ridiculous. It looked like a jacket that Lionel Richie would have worn in the eighties. It was this white leather jacket with big shoulders and because she was teeny, she looked like an upside-down triangle. But she loved it for some reason. I remember she put it on and said, 'Oh, this is beautiful.' It was like two thousand dollars and the saleswoman was kind of giving her attitude like, well, it's very expensive. I said, 'We'll take it,' and my mother had so much fun telling that story. I could have never known that those were the last great fun moments with my mother. It wasn't about the money at all; it was just about being able to give her a freedom that she had never had. That kind of *bon vivant* lifestyle that she had never had because her whole life she had given it to me and to my brother and to my father and everybody else in her life."

On the morning of July 17, Jackie's dad woke her up to say her mother was being taken to the hospital. She had stopped breathing. By the time they got to the hospital, Joyce had slipped into a coma she would never come out of. "I had no idea that she was dying. I thought that she'll get better now that she's in the hospital. She had to get better. But then they finally said she's not going to get better. It's just the worst thing to have to experience. The one thing that I'm grateful for is that we were all there with her and we were telling stories about her life and we were laughing about stuff she did. But it's just the worst. I literally held her head when she took her last breath. It's just the worst thing. The good news is that I had a great mother. My mother was my best friend. She was my rock. But when the rock is gone, you are just floating around going, 'Okay, now where do I anchor?' There's so many things I feel like I didn't find out, like I didn't get the recipe for certain dishes and I don't know what to do in certain situations, and she won't be here when I become a mother. How do I do that without her?"

Jackie recalls receiving a call from her mother when she saw her on television one day. "You know, I just wanted to call you because I'm watching you on television and I'm sitting here thinking, 'Where did she get that sparkle?'" Confused, Jackie asked, "What are you talking about? Are you talking about my hair, because I have that gloss in my hair?" And her mother replied, "No. Look at you; you are funny, you are smart, and you just have this sparkle. I just don't

know where you get it." Jackie laughed and said, "Well, Mom, you are my mother. Of course you think that." But Joyce insisted, "You sure don't get that sparkle from your dad and you surely don't get it from me. Jacksie (her mother was the only person who ever called her Jacksie), I've really done my job with you because when you talk to people, you make them feel important and you can say things that they don't necessarily want to hear, but you make them laugh."

Today, Jackie says, "I can honestly say that if I die tomorrow, I've lived the life I want. Except for the fact that I don't have my mother physically with me anymore and I guess that in the scheme of things, I had her when I really needed her. But at the same time, it's very hard for me not to have my mother. People always say that things get easier in time but it's not really true. It's just that eventually you get busy, so you don't necessarily have time to sit around and cry and look at pictures every day." ∎

Dreams Come True

Christina Vidal

AND HER MOTHER,

Josephine Vidal

As an accomplished singer and actress, Christina Vidal is very much like the title character she plays in Nickelodeon's hit comedy series *Taina*. But unlike her television character, who wants to break into show business, Christina has been a working actress since she was twelve years old. After making her film debut starring opposite Michael J. Fox in *Life with Mikey*, Christina has been working nonstop. ■ Christina's mother, Josefine Vidal ("Josie"), raised Christina and her other talented siblings in Queens, New York, a long way from her native Puerto Rico. Josie proudly points to her daughter's life and success as proof that dreams are worth sacrificing for.

DREAMS COME TRUE

When Josie Vidal heard that her daughter was up for the lead role in the Nickelodeon series *Taina,* she told her daughter, "Ay, Mami, you have to get this part. This would be such a wonderful opportunity for you. I know it." Christina Vidal says that when it comes to career advice her mother is always right. "My mother is so spiritually connected that she gets feelings and she tells me when something's good and when something's not good for me. She told me, 'Mamita, this is a great opportunity for you and a great show. A television show where you get to be a role model for young Latina girls is not only a privilege but something you have to take very serious.' So I said, 'Okay, I'm going to bust my butt on this audition.' "

Once again, Josie's feelings were proved right and Christina got the part. *Taina* turned out to be a top-rated and award-winning show that brought a lot of attention to the young star. But Christina always remembers that behind her success is the hard work and sacrifice of her mother.

Like the three daughters and one son she raised, Josie was born with dreams and talent. And like her daughters, Josie loved to sing and dance. Christina says, "She used to tell me stories about how she would sneak off to the clubs when she was a teenager and she would just dance all night. She was an amazing dancer; even my father told me she was an amazing dancer. And last year she actually started writing poems and giving me ideas for songs for my new album. Without a doubt, I owe a lot of my creativity and talent to her."

Josie has encouraged creativity in all of her children. Out of her four children, Josie has three daughters who are working actors. Her oldest daughter, Lisa Vidal, stars in *The Division* and *E.R.* And the youngest, Tanya Vidal, also appears in *The Division.* But the freedom her daughters have to pursue their careers came at a high cost to their mother.

"I don't know how she did it," Christina says. "She is a selfless person and because of that, I was given the opportunity to be selfish. My mother's devotion to her children allowed us to say, 'This is what I want to do with my life and this is what's going to make me happy.' But I don't think my mother ever had the opportunity to say that. Nobody ever asked her, 'What do you want to do? What's going to make you happy?' "

Christina describes her mother as one of the most giving people she knows, sometimes at the expense of her own desires. "She's used to doing things for other people. She's used to not caring about herself or what she wants to do. In order to do things like superwoman, you can't have time for yourself. At the end of the day my mom loves her children and she loves her family and she's happy when we're happy but she's not a happy person. She's not fulfilled on a personal level. She's not a person who experienced life and love and all those things you should experience growing up. She never had the opportunity to do that. That always makes me sad."

<hr />

JOSIE WAS BORN in Puerto Rico but was brought to New York when she was four years old. Despite the fact that she came to the United States at a young age, Josie did not speak English well until she was in high school because her mother only spoke Spanish to her.

She came from a family of sixteen kids, and most of her siblings were divided up among other relatives to be raised. Josie lived with her mother, two sisters, and a brother. As the oldest child, it fell on Josie's shoulders to raise the other children. Christina explains, "I don't think my mother has ever had a childhood. I don't think she's ever gone through the normal stages of childhood or adolescence. She's been a mother and the head of the household since she was a little girl. She started working in factories at ten years old and she would have to bring the checks to my grandmother and then take care of the kids. My grandmother was never home because she was out partying. My mother had to be a mother, a father, and a sister. She had to be everything to her siblings. She is still like that to this day.

"She definitely regrets not having a childhood. She and I constantly battle about this because she doesn't understand everything that I go through because she's never been given the opportunity to go through it. To her, everything is about responsibility and she's had to be responsible since she was ten years old. So when she talks to me, she can't imagine not having responsibility. I think she has a lot of resentment towards her mother and even towards her siblings. I think she's definitely resentful. She never got to follow her dreams, she never got to do anything she loved to do, and she never had the opportunity to seek out what made her happy."

While Josie had to work and watch over her sisters and brother, she also

Josie Vidal surrounded by her daughters, Tanya, Lisa, and Christina Vidal.

had to go to school. She remained in school, advancing all the way to her senior year in high school. It was at that point she met Christina's father and she dropped out of school to marry him. Within a year, Josie had her first child. She escaped from one house full of responsibility only to get married and find herself in another house full of responsibility. "She told me that she married my father to escape the life she was living, but she just went from one responsibility to the next. In retrospect she feels that was her biggest mistake—she doesn't regret having her children, but she regrets never having had time for herself. She's always drilling me about that because she feels like it was something she really missed out on."

Josie wants to make sure that her daughters don't repeat her mistake and saddle themselves with the obligations of marriage and children before they have the opportunity to live out their dreams. "Her biggest concern for her children is that we don't have to go through what she went through. She missed out on her life and had to struggle a lot more than if she would have waited."

While Josie has sacrificed much, she has also gained much. "The best way to put it is we are her life," Christina explains. "Everything that involves us, everything that we feel, everything that we go through, she is there to support us every step of the way. And if nobody else is cheering for us, she will be our cheerleader. She'll be the first person to drag everybody along to our performances and say, 'You have to see my kids!' She and my dad are very, very proud, not in an obnoxious way, but in a way that's very endearing. You just look at them and see that they really love their children."

And as the focus of her life, Josie paid close attention to her baby daughter and noticed that she was talented from a very young age. "She used to take pictures of me when I was dressed up in her clothes. From the beginning she knew I was interested in performing, so she enrolled me in singing lessons when I was nine."

Unlike many child stars whose parents sometimes force them into the limelight for all the wrong reasons, Josie waited for Christina to express an interest in performing before enrolling her in classes. "What's so beautiful about my mother is that she would always ask me if I wanted to do something. I was never forced into anything. She noticed I had an interest in dancing or singing and then she would look for a class. She would ask me, 'Do you want to take this class? And I'd do it. She wouldn't force me to do anything, but she would make sure that once I started something, that I stayed with it.

"She was very big on keeping me busy during my summertime so I didn't have free time to get into trouble. She took me to ballet when I was five years old, because she said from when I was a baby that I was always so dramatic. Once she realized that I wasn't really into ballet, she took me out of it and then enrolled me in singing lessons."

As supportive as she was, Josie nearly let Christina's big break in the Michael J. Fox movie *Life with Mikey* slip away from her when she was ten years old. "What's funny about that is that she didn't want to take me to the audition. I brought this paper home from my school and I was like, 'Mommy, Mommy, I want to audition for this. They said it was a cool movie.' But she said, '*Ay*, Christina *por favor*,

Josie Vidal with her daughter,
Christina Vidal.

me. My parents were shocked that I got a callback for the movie, and when I got the lead in the movie, my mother knew I had a knack for this. So from then on, she took the initiative in my career. She made sure I had an agent and made sure that I got to all my auditions. She was just superwoman. She went to work, ran her household, found a way to get me to my auditions and make sure I stayed in school and did everything I was supposed to do all while taking care of four children. She was just amazing."

Josie was equally amazed at her daughter. When Christina won the title role in *Taina*, Josie was incredibly proud that her daughter's presence on television opened up new doors for Latinas. "She would remind me that I was a role model for young girls, especially Latinas who dare to follow their dreams."

Josie has encouraged all her daughters in the same way. "She's always telling Lisa that she loves the character that she plays in *The Division* because it is strong. Because my mother is such a strong woman, she likes for us to be represented in that way. Lisa had to do so many crappy jobs when she first started out in this business and my mom used to always encourage her. She would tell her not to worry because

I cannot be running you around to auditions, I have to go to work, your father's busy and I don't know how we're going to get you there. You need to just go to school and forget about it.' I cried, I cried, I cried and so finally she called my older sister, Lisa, who was already in the business at this point. She said, 'Mira, Lisa, this little girl is driving me crazy. She wants to go on this audition. I don't know what this is or what's going on.' She gave Lisa the paper; Lisa read it and said it was a great opportunity. So Lisa took over from there and got me ready for the audition.

"She worked with me and took me to the audition. Every audition I had for *Life with Mikey* Lisa was there, coaching she will get better parts. She would tell her, 'It's not you, it's the ignorance of the people in the business.' She always had the right things to say to keep us moving."

Christina and her sisters strongly feel that they would not be the women they are without their mother's love and support. "She equipped us with the strength and the confidence to go out there and do what we want to do. I think that it takes love and support and a good plate of rice and beans. There's nothing like some of my mother's rice and beans and pork chops to just make you forget about a bad audition."

Josie could not be happier that her daughters are doing what they love to do. "It's almost like she feels like it's worth everything that she's ever gone through because she looks at her children and sees that they're happy and settled and they have everything she never had. She feels like she's accomplished her life's mission."

Now that her children are grown and living their own lives, Josie has been trying to figure out what she wants to do with her own life. "For the last two years I've been trying to encourage her to figure out what she really wants," Christina explains. "I want her to be selfish and figure out what would make her happy, whether it's going off to an island for three weeks or taking a painting class. Her answer to everything is, 'I'll be happy when my children are settled and happy.' " But Christina insists that she wants her mother to find some type of happiness that is outside of her children. "I don't think it's too late, although she does. She has a young spirit, which is even more important than the age." ■

Josie Vidal (second from right) is flanked by her daughters, Lisa, Tanya, and Christina.

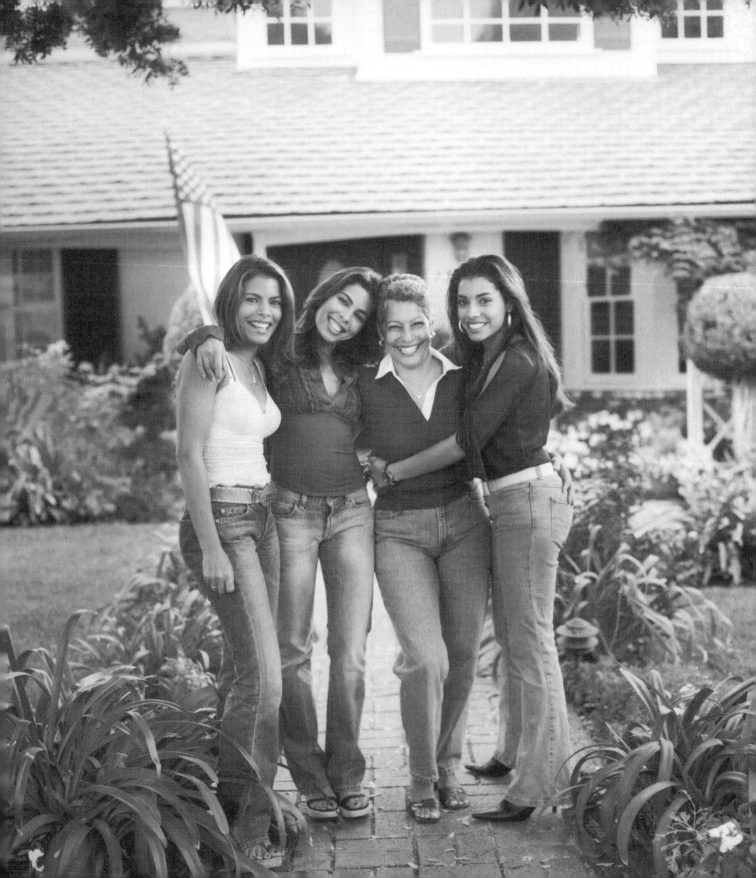

Law and Order

Judge Marilyn Milian

AND HER MOTHER,

Georgina Milian

Judge Marilyn Milian is more than a judge—she's the judge on the nationally syndicated television series *The People's Court.* But long before she started pounding the gavel on the popular courtroom series, she was pounding the gavel as an appointee to the Miami Circuit Court, where she served in the criminal division. Marilyn was also hired by Janet Reno to serve as an assistant state attorney for the Dade County State Attorney's Office. ■ While her accomplishments are impressive, what impresses Marilyn the most is the woman who made it all possible: her mother, Georgina.

LAW AND ORDER

WHEN MARILYN MILIAN was five years old, a teacher told her parents that their daughter was going to be a lawyer. However, it wasn't until she was in college studying psychology that she decided to face her teacher's prediction. "I thought I would go on to graduate school in psychology and then become a psychologist. But my mother sat me down and said, 'You know, you're a much better talker than you are a listener, maybe you ought to think about being a lawyer.' Which is not a great thing for a judge to be, unless you're a TV judge."

Marilyn credits Georgina for not only encouraging her to make the leap into law, but for giving her the gifts of opportunity and freedom. "I ended up working in an internship with the state attorney's office. I found it fascinating and I decided I wanted to go to law school because I wanted to be a prosecutor. What my mother did for me was to encourage me all of my life. I was in college to pick the right thing for myself, but she showed what the right thing was by encouraging me.

"My mother was one of these mothers who would basically put her entire life on hold for her children. I mean, she didn't work, she stayed at home, and she raised her kids, which is something that might not be economically feasible for the women of today to choose to do. But I am able to choose not to do it because she chose to do it. That's how I was able to attend good schools. That's how I was able to stay on top of my studies. That's how I was able to do everything I did, because of everything that she did. She made sure that I came from an intact home and that I wasn't strapped with all those student loans. She was minding the house while my father was out there working, and they provided the opportunity for me to do absolutely everything that I was able to do.

"Both of my parents considered that college was the thirteenth grade. You were going. It's not like either one of my parents ever thought, 'Well, we want her to be a nice housewife.' What they did think was, 'What she needs is to find a nice man.' They always wanted me to find a nice man and they were pretty worried when at thirty-two I hadn't gotten married. But they both stressed education and a career. So in that sense, they weren't traditional. A lot of people think that college isn't considered for a girl in a Cuban household. But in my house it always was. Both kids were going to college, that's all there was to it."

When it came to dating though, Marilyn remembers how she and her brother were treated somewhat differently. Her brother was given not only a different curfew but also a different set of dating standards. "My parents were traditionally Cuban. They had a certain demeanor or decorum about dating and all that. Hispanic parents train their boys to be the kind of boys they want to keep their daughters away from. It's like, 'You go, boy!' when they're out there. But the rules are different for the girls.

"Do you think my brother got chaperoned? The worst was when they had my brother chaperone me. I don't even want to talk about that. I said I'd rather go out with Dad than my brother. He was the worst. He would bark at my dates all the time. It was the worst!"

Marilyn recalls when her mother drove her to her first day of school for her senior year of high school. "I was president of the student council, which meant you had all these responsibilities to put on many functions, including the prom, but I wasn't allowed to be in a car with other teenagers unless an adult was there. As we drove in to school, I said to my mother, 'It's the first day of school, I want you to tell me you're going to lay off the chaperone concept. If you're not going to lay off, I'm going to march right into the office and I'm going to resign as president of the student council. I'm a senior in high school. It cannot go on.' She just laughed. She knew she had pushed it as far as she could and it was over. After that I was actually able to be in cars with other children during daylight hours.

These days Marilyn sees similarities to her mother in some of the most important areas of her life. "My mother will sit there and laugh when she sees my husband. She says, 'He's exactly like your father.' My husband even looked like my father, before he had gray hair. My father is a very handsome man, too. I very much married my father.

"My husband jokes that I subscribe to *Fretful Mother* magazine because I worry about everything when it comes to my kids. I'm in tune with everything. My house is very matriarchal. In my mother's house, my mother called all the shots, too. I mean, my father was happy to leave the reins to her, he would wash the big pots and say, 'I do big pots and big decisions.' Everything else my mother ran."

One way that Marilyn did not follow in her mother's footsteps is in her career. For that, Marilyn had to forge her own, unique path from the courtroom to the television studio. "I wasn't looking to get in this business at all. The way they found me was my neighbor auditioned for this job. They wanted to change the direction of the show and they were looking for

Georgina Milian and her daughter, Judge Marilyn Milian.

a Latina. So they were looking in all the cities where Latinos congregate. Somebody knew somebody who knew my neighbor who's not a judge, but she's a Latina lawyer in Miami. So she auditioned and said to them, 'Look, I don't know if you're going to call me back, but you've gotta call my neighbor.' And she gave them my name. One of the executive producers of *The People's Court* called and I didn't call him back because I was in the middle of a first-degree murder trial. He was very persistent. After a couple of calls I finally called the producer back and we set up an audition. They brought me up a second time with my husband and they told me to get an agent. I'm so naive because I said I didn't need an agent or a lawyer, because my husband and I are both lawyers. They said, 'Please, we don't want to take advantage of you, get an agent.' And I did.

"Being a judge on television is different from being a real judge in the sense that it gives me a chance to take the handcuffs off. People don't watch the show to watch me think, they want to *hear* me think, they want to hear what's on my mind. And so I get to say what's on my mind constantly, which is frankly very invigorating and very liberating. To me, in a sense, it's much easier than what I was doing before, because not only do I get to say what's on my mind, but my producer insists upon it."

Growing up in Miami, Marilyn remembers her mother making their house the center of activities and celebrations. "Everybody's birthday, every Father's Day and Mother's Day, every Easter everyone is expected to go over to the *abuelos* and celebrate. That still goes on now and sometimes I have to remind my mom that I am forty years old and that my husband also has a family that we have to share time with on different holidays."

Another part of the Milian family tradition was that Marilyn and her brother were expected to speak Spanish. "There was no question for my mother that we were going to speak Spanish. And I struggle with that with my kids. My husband is fluent in Spanish even though he's not Hispanic. He minored in Spanish and lived in Spain. We were really good about teaching our children Spanish in the beginning and then the children started to watch television and go to school. They started picking up English so much faster that we have to really concentrate to make sure that they speak Spanish. We'll speak in Spanish to them and try to get them to speak the language. It's just difficult at this age when they're grasping so much in English and they don't want to learn Spanish.

"My parents used to speak to us in Spanish all the time, and when we answered them in English they would say, 'Speak to me in Spanish.' Now they're speaking English to their grandkids, which is what they didn't do to us. We have a nanny who helps us out and she only speaks in Spanish to them."

When it comes to her own children, Marilyn isn't certain how much like her mother she will be to her daughters. "Each generation hopefully tends to perfect their concept of parenting. There's a saying, 'Oh, God, I'm becoming my mother,' or 'I am my mother.' And although I'm struck by the similarities between my mother and me, I will not chaperone my daughters. I will put a lot more trust in their judgment than my mom put in mine. I don't fault her, because basically she did as much as she could get away with. She sheltered me as long as she could shelter me.

"When I was applying to law schools, my parents said to me, 'You know you're not going out of state. It's cute that you want to apply to all these schools, but if you get accepted, you're not going away.' My father had some lawyer who said to my parents, 'Are you guys crazy? You can't do that.' "

Marilyn was accepted at Georgetown University Law School and recalls how her mother was adamant that she was not going to let her go away to law school. "It was my birthday and I had been accepted into Georgetown and I said, 'I'm going. I don't know how I was going to pay for it, but I'm going, I'm going, I'm going.' My parents were saying, 'You're not going.' And then in a birthday card, my mother wrote, 'We are letting you go.' And I was so happy.

"I think Latina women, at least of our mothers' generation, think the value in an item is the value that others place on it. When I got the opportunity to be on *The People's Court* I sat my parents down. My father is a very bottom-line kind of guy; he was like, 'You go, girl!' He's high-fiving me. He was so excited for me. My mother was a little horrified, she was like, 'But is this more prestigious?' and 'Are you gonna give up this gubernatorial appointment?' My mother had very mixed emotions. Then when the show aired and friend after friend would come up to her and say, 'Your daughter's great,' she'd say, 'Yeah, that's my daughter.' When she'd see commercials, she'd say, 'That's my daughter.' All of a sudden it was a great idea.

"When I think about my mother I'm overcome with a sense of 'You go, girl.' My mother doesn't make up the professional side of me, although she gave me the liberty to go ahead and do all those things by providing the home that they provided. You are an adult, but the core of your being, your ethics, come from the kind of mother you had. Who you are comes to you by what you saw, the mothering you saw in your household. The kind of person you are, whether you're honest, whether you're good to other people, whether you are selfless, whether you are kind, all those things are things that my mother created in me.

"People may look at me and say, 'Oh, she got this job on *The People's Court*,' or 'Oh, she was a judge,' or 'Oh, she got this gubernatorial appointment.' What they don't see is how I snagged a great guy and I snagged him because of the woman that I am. And I am that woman because of the woman that made me. I am raising beautiful children because of the woman that made me. Those are the true successes of my life." ■

The Power Behind the Throne

Denise Quiñones

AND HER MOTHER,

Susana August de Quiñones

When Denise Quiñones entered her very first beauty competition, she was crowned Miss Puerto Rico. From there, the native of Lares, Puerto Rico, won the title of Miss Universe, 2001. In high school, Denise danced professionally for the daily variety show *El Super Show* and cohosted a weekly variety show, *Eso Vale*, in Puerto Rico. ■ Following her string of successes is her mother and friend, Susana August de Quiñones. Susana proudly channels her creativity and energy into her family and, especially, the life of her daughter.

THE POWER BEHIND THE THRONE

Upon meeting Denise Quiñones it becomes apparent why the nineteen-year-old Puerto Rican beauty queen won the 2001 Miss Universe crown—she has impressive beauty, charisma, intelligence, and poise. Since the Miss Universe contest began fifty years ago, fifteen Latin American women (including Denise) have won the crown. Denise is the fourth Puerto Rican to win the highly competitive contest. One thing distinguished Denise from the other contestants—unlike the many who typically began competing in beauty contests while they were still wearing diapers, Denise didn't begin competing until she was at the ripe old age of seventeen. The person responsible for her unofficial "training" is her mother, Susana August de Quiñones.

"Pageants didn't begin to interest me until I was seventeen years old," explains Denise. "I started out being interested in modeling. I competed in a Hispanic Model Search competition for JCPenney. There were sixteen participants and we had two months over the summer when they would teach us the basics. I never had classes in modeling, walking, or photography before, so it was a crash course." But it was a crash course that paid off. Denise won the competition in Puerto Rico, and then won the national competition in Texas against young women representing all of the other JCPenney stores in the United States. Having had her first taste of pageant success and curious to see how far she could go, Denise decided to compete the following year for Miss Puerto Rico, representing her hometown of Lares.

Growing up in Lares, Denise remembers that her mother was always involved in everything she and her brother did. "I believe it was her mission to keep us together and give us the happiest childhood she could possibly give us."

Denise remembers vividly the birthday parties her mother would throw. "Because my brother was born in August and I was born in September, we celebrated our birthdays together. Our birthdays were like the celebration of the year for us because we invited the entire extended family and all our friends. It was a great big family reunion!"

Susana would work for months preparing for these elaborate birthday parties. "My mother is really creative and would design and make souvenirs for our parties. She would make little rag dolls for the children. She would be at it for weeks and weeks, making those dolls, souvenirs, and little candy gifts. She would decorate the house and make up games and activities for all the guests. One time she made up a game where she brought a whole bunch of clothes from her closet and my father's closet and she would put them in a bundle. The children and even the grown-ups would have to run, put on all the clothes, and then take them off. And the one who would do it the fastest would be the winner. And she would always have the prizes for the winners. They were incredible birthdays!"

Susana was born in California, the child of Native American, Puerto Rican, Mexican, and German ancestry. After the divorce of her parents, Susana moved with her mother to Ponce, Puerto Rico, where they lived with her grandparents. Moving to Puerto Rico at fifteen years old was difficult for her. "My mother spoke only English when she got to Puerto Rico. She had to take classes all over again, taking Spanish and other classes a grade beneath her. But she learned how to speak Spanish really fast.

"My mom lived with her mother and all her sisters. She had nine or ten brothers and sisters. My dad lived on the same street as my mom. She always told us stories about how they used to call my dad El Gallo [the rooster] because he used to sing. My father always had his guitar and he hung out with a bunch of women who lived across the street from where my mother lived." Denise laughs and says, "He was always there playing the guitar with all those women around him singing. So that's where my parents met."

After a courtship of six or seven months, the couple married. Shortly thereafter, Denise was born, followed by her brother. More than a mother, Susana took on the role of coordinating all of her children's activities. "Ever since kindergarten, she was the one that always organized the talent shows for us and the other students in my school. Every Christmas there was a recital in school and all the groups had to present something creative. And Mom would always be in charge of helping us create things. She was always really active and involved in everything her children did." During this time Susana also worked as a secretary for the Puerto Rico Telephone company in Ponce. Later,

when the family moved to Lares, she and her husband opened a pet shop, which she ran.

Susana would support her children in anything they expressed an interest in. "I always wanted to dance and she was one of the first people to support me. When I was about seven years old, I wanted to study at a local dance academy. But ever since I was a little girl, my father has been the one who has been more resistant to things like that. For him, education was the most important thing because that's how he was raised. There has always been that little struggle with him. He was afraid that I would be distracted from my studies. My mom was always the one who would say, 'Yes, she is going to dance classes. Yes, yes, yes!' Dad had been resistant until a few years ago, when he's seen everything I've accomplished. And he has seen that I can do the two things at once because I always kept up with my studies. I was always an honor student and that's always been my challenge.

"But Mom was always the one who would take me every Saturday to dance class. We had recitals called *Lanzares* which was the biggest show in Lares. It happened every year in May or June. And the rehearsals were really strenuous for two weeks before the event. We rehearsed every day from the time we would come out of school at four o'clock till twelve or one in the morning. I remember that I would do my dance and when it was other groups' turn to rehearse, I would do my homework while the music was blaring. And Mom would stay there with me until twelve or one in the morning. Sometimes she went home and came back to bring me dinner. She was always wonderful."

When Denise decided to take the plunge and enter the Miss Puerto Rico contest, her mother was naturally supportive. Denise was surprised to find that the other contestants had teams of professional people helping them with their hair, their makeup, and their studies while all she had was her family. And she discovered that family was enough. "My father and my mother were the ones who would ask me questions in preparation for the contest so that I could get more comfortable and loose. They would sit down with me in the living room and ask me questions and I would answer them."

Denise won the Miss Puerto Rico competition and her mother was the loudest voice in her cheering section. "Mom always gets so emotional. She can hardly talk. She trembles. She shakes, cries, stares, and then she can't say anything. She looks at me and you see this expression of such joy in her eyes. She can't breathe and she starts to cry."

When it came to makeup, hair, and clothing, Denise got her basic training from her mother. "My mother was a simple woman. She would tell me that the secret to beauty is to always have my face clean. She would tell me not to use so many products. Soap was the best. She was very simple, really basic. Mom was always using that Agua Maravilla. My mom was always saying, 'Use Agua Maravilla, use Agua Maravilla.' I never used it because I never liked the smell."

Denise recalls that being presentable has always been important to Susana. "Growing up, when we went to church, my mother would always dress us really, really nice. I always wanted to be more comfortable and wear casual clothes, but she would tell us that going to God's house was a celebration and in order to show Him respect, we had to be real presentable.

Denise Quiñones embraces her mother, Susana August de Quiñones.

But it was always a battle with me and my brother to get us to dress up.

"When I was a little girl, she used to brush my hair for me and put it in two little ponytails or one big ponytail on the side. I always remember the image of my mother brushing my hair because I had so much. When I danced in the recitals, she would always do my makeup for me. I never used makeup to go to school, not even when I was in twelfth grade. If there was a party, in the tenth, eleventh, or twelfth grade, I used a little makeup. But I never used makeup to go to school."

Susana is an active woman and expected her daughter to be active too. Anything was better than sitting at home and watching television. "I think she would worry if I had nothing to do. She really believes in extracurricular activities. She made sure I had too much to do. I was involved in everything and she was there to support me in everything I did. My brother was into soccer, and my mom and I would follow his bus in our car to his games. She dedicated her whole life to us."

When Denise entered the Miss Universe Pageant as Miss Puerto Rico, she learned that some changes were expected. Instead of her family being the team that helped her, a group of professionals took charge of everything. "I took makeup and hair styling classes every day for two hours. Every morning from six to eight I would work out doing cardiovascular and weights. And, depending on the day, I had dance classes or modeling classes, diction classes, and classes on public speaking. I had English classes in the morning, singing classes, appointments with designers and different people throughout the day." These were really intense months for Denise because she still had to continue her activities as Miss Puerto Rico. "As Miss Puerto Rico, I still had to visit institutions, be with kids, and film commercials.

"During that time, I lived in San Juan. It was a difficult time because I had never really been away from home. I would try to go home to be with my family on weekends, but many weekends I didn't get to go. I had to stay in San Juan all week. During that period, I really didn't get to see my family a lot."

The days of preparing for the Miss Universe contest were difficult not only for Denise but also for her mother. They had never spent such a long period of time apart and it was stressful. But finally, all of the long months of preparation and separation came to an end and it was time for the contest. After her mother stayed up all night packing her bags in her apartment, Denise headed off to San Juan for the Miss Universe Pageant.

"I called her every day. I would call home from the hotel and I would ask her about everything, like, 'How did I look in that magazine?' 'How did I look in the show last night?' 'How did I sound during the interview?' I would always ask for her opinion. And she would tell me, 'Good,' or 'Bad,' or 'Change this.' She would give me her opinion and great advice. It was beautiful."

Susana has ten scrapbooks and albums filled with all of the newspaper articles about Denise—not only of the Miss Universe contest but of Miss Puerto Rico and her performances as a dancer in high school. "She has collected everything you can imagine. And she has a whole wall of VHS videos of all the appearances I've made on television. She has a videotape in the VCR ready at any given moment, just in case I happen to be on TV. She just pushes a button and records it."

Denise laughs. "For a week after I won Miss Universe, she would play the video for everyone that came to my house. And when I come out in a magazine or a newspaper, she buys them all, keeps one or two for herself, and the rest of them she sends to different members of my family. She sends my grandfather who lives in the United States a box filled with everything I've done every month or so. She's like that."

As Miss Universe, Denise has travelled around the world, falling in love with places far beyond the shores of her home-town. As she visits various countries, she acts as an ambassador for Miss Universe by raising international awareness of the treatment and prevention of the AIDS epidemic. Denise takes her role seriously and accepts the responsibility of being a role model, particularly for Latinas. "The little girls I meet see me as an example to follow. It's really nice, but it's a great responsibility as well." Denise wants to continue being a role model for girls as she pursues her singing and acting career beyond the reign of Miss Universe.

As Denise's reign as Miss Universe comes to an end, she has dreams of becoming a recording artist and hosting her own television show. As she weighs her many possibilities, she's clear on one thing: "Of course I'm going home first.

My family is counting the days until I come home and I mark on my calendar every day that passes. My family knows that I am going home for a while but, at the same time, they know that I will be doing something else in the future."

Denise feels that all the lights, cameras, and action surrounding the Miss Universe Pageant has not affected her relationship with her mother. They were close before the excitement and will remain so after she relinquishes her crown. "I'm grateful to her for dedicating her life, not only to me but to my brother and father as well. She has been a pillar of strength in the beautiful bond that we as a family share. She's dedicated all her life to us, all her strength and all her energy was for us, and I will always thank her for it. I see her not only as a mother but also as a woman that I admire because she gives in ways that I never would imagine." ∎

Denise Quiñones strikes a pose with her mother, Susana August de Quiñones.

The Gift of Giving

Kim Flores

AND HER MOTHER,

Amelia Flores

Kim Flores is a filmmaker whose short film *Maid! Madonna! Whore! The Latina in American Cinema!* says a lot about Kim. It's funny, loud, brightly colored, and relevant. Kim brings this quirky sensibility to all of her film projects (her *Vocessitas/Little Voices*, won the ALMA Award for Outstanding Independent Feature). She also brings this quality to her life. ■ Kim is part of the fifth generation of Florcses to be born and raised in Texas. The fact that she was named after the Kimberley diamond mine in South Africa demonstrates that she was an unusual child born of unusual Mexican-American parents. And everything Kim has she got from her mother, Amelia Flores. Being the mother of six children, Amelia has had to lean on her own brand of quirkiness not only to survive but to thrive.

THE GIFT OF GIVING

One day last spring, Kim received a frantic call from her sister informing her that their mother, Amelia, had just suffered a heart attack. She was barely fifty-seven years old. This was an event that changed Amelia's relationship with her family forever.

"I had just come back from Portland and my sister told me Mom had a heart attack," recalls Kim. The second-oldest of six children, Kim immediately got on the phone and rallied all the siblings together. "I had a three-hour drive to get to the hospital from where I live and in my mind I was already preparing her funeral. I thought about what I would say and do. My mom writes poetry, so I thought about the poems I would read and what songs I would play. Mom likes these crazy songs like 'Love Won't Hurt Anymore' from *The Love Boat* and 'I Can't Smile Without You' from Barry Manilow. Everything was rushing in my head. Then I thought, 'No. I want her to see me get married and I want her to see me have babies.' I know those were selfish reasons, but I started bartering with God, going, 'Please, please, I'll be really, really good this time.'"

By the time Kim arrived at the hospital, her family had already gathered around her mother. "I saw her laying there unconscious. It reminded me of my own mortality. We all reacted differently as a family. Some of us wanted to be there all the time; some needed their distance because it was overwhelming. Some of us had to stay busy; some wanted to take a nap. But it was just amazing how we all came together. It was like holding your breath for days and days and days.

"A lot of the time she wasn't conscious and we learned how fragile the body could be. The doctors had to watch her blood pressure and her heart rate. They put her on a ventilating tube so she could breathe and they had to give her a feeding tube, but the feeding tube leaked into her lungs and they had to suction it out and that gave her an infection. Things would change every hour on the hour and we were just watching and waiting. The funny thing was because she's "brown," people would ask, 'Does she speak English?' I wanted to put up a big sign on the door saying this woman has her masters in English and she's bilingual. She can answer in anything."

It is usually during trying times like these, when we are facing life-and-death situations, that we reach deep within and recall the lessons passed down to us by our mothers. Standing by Amelia's hospital bed, Kim remembered one of the most valuable lessons she got from her mother: Never lose your faith.

"Faith has been a thread throughout

my mother's life and that has been instilled in us as well. Faith is about believing in what you cannot see. When she gave birth to me she had complications. First the doctors thought she had bad gas and they told her she wasn't pregnant. But my mom said, 'I had one of these before, so I know what this is.' They told her she just needed to drink more water because she was probably constipated. When they found out that I existed, the doctors instructed her to terminate the pregnancy because of problems with her kidneys. She refused. There were three doctors telling her to do it because it could be life threatening. She told them, 'Well, you know what? You're not God and you can't speak His mind and if something were to happen, He'll let me know. I just got to go through with this.' "

Amelia went on to give birth to a healthy baby girl she named Kimberley. Unfortunately, the birth created problems with her kidneys. "The problems with my mother's kidneys became a bigger problem when she had her heart attack." Expressing her sense of guilt, Kim explains, "I have that little feeling of responsibility. I feel really grateful, because she let me come into existence even though it hurt her down the line."

Born in Corpus Christi, Texas, Amelia Flores came from a large family with a very spiritual mother. She was raised in the Catholic faith. But when Amelia decided that she wanted to become a nun, her parents refused to give her permission because she was the youngest. Her friends also made fun of her, asking why she would want to be a nun. Coincidentally, her two best friends later became nuns. Despite her initial career choice, Amelia embraced her new role as wife and mother.

"She instilled in all of us that you can always do anything you want to do. Anything is possible if you believe in yourself and if you believe in a higher power. She told us, 'There's people out there beyond what we can see that are watching.' She always made life out to be like this journey and we're all getting on a bus that's headed to somewhere better. But what's hard sometimes is that when it's time to get off at our stop, we don't want to go and we want to stay here. But this isn't our final destination.

"I think when she had her heart attack we knew she was getting close to that. We said, 'Whatever you want, God, we will accept. Whatever you decide. We know that she has lived a good lifetime with us. We know that she loves us. She knows that we love her and that we want her here, but what is the lesson we are to learn here?' And so, when times get tough, when we don't know what to do, we stop and we just learn to be quiet. We just listen to whatever is out there that will lead us to what we are supposed to learn while going through these trials."

Kim Flores and her mother, Amelia Flores.

This lesson was never tested more than during the hours she spent waiting in the hospital. The hours felt like they would never end. "Somebody came up with the idea of going down to the chapel. The chapel was a real quiet place where we could hang out. We all held hands and talked about the things that our mother instilled in us and what we learned during her life, especially now that she could be here or she could not.

"We remembered all the crazy things we did together. We laughed about the time our mother was in a hurry making chorizo and wasn't paying attention. Instead of putting in the oil she put in dishwashing soap, like she was trying to kill us! We talked about how she taught us all to uplift and take care of each other in the good and bad times. No matter what, she was always gonna be with us and she was with us right then. We were holding hands and, even though she was a couple floors above us, we felt her love in all of us. It was like we didn't want to let go. That's when we knew she had done a good job with all of us. It didn't matter what careers we had, what mattered was that we had each other and with that we could get through anything. After we left the chapel we felt really, really calm. It's almost like she came and she made everything better again."

But it wasn't always that harmonious for the Flores family. Kim's parents went through difficult periods in their marriage. Her father's work in education demanded long hours and constantly kept him on the road. Amelia had the primary responsibility for raising their children. "I think my mother learned she had a great strength that she didn't know that she had. My parent's marriage was rocky at times but my mother always kept it together for the family to a point, I think, that the stress hurt her health. There were times when we wanted her to get a divorce because we figured they would be happier separated, but somehow they just came spiraling back together. I think we were the only kids during the seventies who wanted their mother and father to get a divorce.

"I remember when I was five and my dad was packing up his stuff to live in his own apartment. He had his drawer of clothes and I jerked it out of his hands and said, 'Nobody's leaving, nowhere, nohow.' But when I was fifteen I was like, 'Let's help him pack.' I think we always wanted to be a family and so it's kind of like this love-craziness that you just want to bring it back and keep it together."

But it was also during the time Amelia was hospitalized for her heart attack that Kim began to see her father in a different light. "The time when my mom got really sick was when my father grew the strongest. It was the first time I saw my father cry in my life and that's why I felt we were okay. If her one task in life was to raise good kids and to turn my father's life around, she did her job and she was ready to go. It's like she kept the string going through us to keep us united."

Kim says she gets her sense of humor and her creativity directly from her mother. "She taught us how to cope through laughter at all times, even in the darkest times. So I think we all have that peculiar sense of humor just to get through the rough times. She's the one who taught us how to make up stories when the TV would get accidentally broken in some skirmish. She encouraged us to do puppet shows. When we had to go on a family trip and be hauled in a station wagon for an eight-hour drive to Corpus, she's the one who dealt out drawing pads. She was a big part of our creative force. She liked to sing and write stories and she encouraged us to do the same. That's where I get my love of writing.

"She also taught us to honor our bodies and to wait to have sex because you can get excited in the moment but then that moment is gone. I think she was trying to make us aware that those feelings that you have are real—'It's like burning fire,' she said, 'but if you can wait and give yourself time to think, then you can cool down and figure it out.' That was a hard lesson.

When Kim was sixteen years old, she found herself going through a hard time because her boyfriend at the time was pressuring her to have sex and she refused. When another girl told Kim that she had sex with Kim's boyfriend, she was devastated. "I didn't want to undergo the hardships in life and love that my mother underwent, so I started cutting myself on my arms. I used to be a 'cutter' and that was before I knew what it was. That was before it was fashionable and on *Oprah*."

Cutting is the most common expression of a self-injuring disorder that also includes burning, self-hitting, hair pulling, bone breaking, and not allowing wounds to heal. It is estimated that there are about two million people in the United States who engage in some form of this behavior. Seventy percent of self-injurers are women, mostly between the ages of eleven and twenty-six, and they come from all races and social classes.

Kim began cutting herself shortly after the incident with her boyfriend. "It pretty much lasted for about five years—cutting is very common if you have eating disorders or if you come from a very stressful, highly dysfunctional family, it's kind of a way to feel. It gets you to focus on something else.

"I got caught cutting in school. I was cleaning up my arm and bleeding in the sink when somebody saw it and ran and told the counselor. So then the nurse took me home and told my parents. They didn't know what to call it so they said

your daughter is trying to kill herself, which wasn't really true, but my mom took it serious regardless of what it was.

"I knew it just upset my mom so much. She said, 'Here, I want to give you life. I think you have so much to offer and I don't want you to go through this tough time and think that this is all there is to life.' She validated everything by saying, 'I know that this is a hard time for you and I know that this boy probably cares for you a whole lot, but there's a lot that's good outside all this. You just wait and keep praying and just believing and do something good for yourself. Just get through the day one minute at a time, one second at a time.' It hurt me to see her hurt. That's the most painful thing I can even imagine.

"My mom always wants to keep communications open. Even to this day, if things are getting kind of rocky, she's like, 'How's it going? Are

*Kim Flores kisses her mother,
Amelia Flores.*

wanted to get some chicken. There was a black girl in the back and a white girl in the front and an older white woman behind the counter. When we ordered our food, she just looked at us. I said, 'Maybe she didn't hear us.' So we said it louder. It was really weird because this was the seventies. Mom said, 'We need to go right now.' I said we were being discriminated against and she said, 'You know what? It's okay. We just need to keep them in our prayers because they don't understand.' And that's how she taught us to deal with difficult situations, always with compassion no matter what. It's like learning to build bridges with people that you don't even think you need because you don't know if later on in life you're going to need them. It's like killing people with kindness because if somebody's having a bad day and you're good to them anyway, then they'll come around and say, 'Oh, I'm sorry, I really had a bad day and I didn't mean it.' You know people will open up their hearts to you if you're kind, if you pray for them, open your heart, and just wait and be still."

Kim and her family grew up in a predominantly white, middle-class neighborhood. "In the seventies we were called Chicanos; in the eighties

you . . . ?' And she'll pat my arm. She still worries about me cutting myself but I haven't done it in a long time. I did it during a little span of time, but you grow out of it. I wanted to be the strong one like she was, but I didn't know how to deal with it."

Another valuable lesson that Amelia instilled in her children was how to handle difficult people. She thought that the best way to deal with people that hurt you was by praying for them "because they don't understand what they do."

Kim recalls one time they we were discriminated against in Garland, Texas, when they went to a KFC (Kentucky Fried Chicken). "We had gone to baton twirling lessons and we we're Mexican-Americans, then Hispanic came along, and now Latin. So now I just say 'brown.' My mother made us very conscious of how other people are raised, and we are privileged to have an education. We learned from her that you should be proud that you're brown, you should be proud of your body, you should be proud of who you are. There is nothing wrong with it, but then at the same time, she loved to dye her hair a million colors. It wasn't that she was trying to be white, but it's also about trying to show who and what you are. Being yourself took courage. But because she was a little bit lighter, a lot of people didn't think that she was brown. I remember she would always laugh because it's like when people found out that she had the name Flores—they'd go, 'You're Mexican. I just love enchiladas.' And she'd give people the benefit of the doubt, knowing they weren't trying to poke fun.

"It was the weirdest thing because we saw miracles with our mother. But when things went dark, when you didn't know where money was for food, she was there for everybody. Sometimes we thought she was crazy. There were times when all we had was pickles and juice in the refrigerator and we'd wonder, 'Now what's gonna happen?' There was one Christmas where we didn't have anything; there was no money. We went to the mall with our mother and she found an envelope with a couple of hundred bucks in it. I told her I wanted to go to Lerner's and buy something and she said, 'We're gonna turn this in.' So we turned it in and as we were leaving the policeman in the mall called her and said, 'You know, nobody came for this money. Why don't you just take it?' Things like that always happened."

Kim thinks her mother's spiritual side partially comes from living in Corpus Christi. "I mean Corpus Christi is called the Body of Christ, for Christ's sake. Mom always had dreams about things beforehand so it's not something that we broadcast a lot to people, like, 'My mother sees dead people.' But there's something bigger than us that we can't see here and it's good and it's watching over us. So when we see something that's peculiar to other people and they think that it's a coincidence, we go, 'Oh, yeah.' "

Amelia taught her daughter many things and has found over the years that she has learned a few things from Kim as well. "My mother's theme has always been about giving. But you shouldn't give so much that you're a pile of ashes and you can't help your family. Don't give so much that you're not taking care of yourself and hurt your own body. I think one of the things we do as women is we learn how to give and give and give and give. But we have a really hard time at giving to ourselves, of taking time for ourselves or taking that bath or whatever. My mother gave so much she sacrificed her health. She wasn't eating right or taking time to exercise. Culturally what we eat is a bit heavy in fats and salts and it's easy to get curvy on a diet of beans and rice. Fast food was another enemy. It bought my mom extra time during her hectic schedule juggling six kids. But over time, that wore her body down.

"Mom always had a beautiful figure until she started getting more kids and she stopped taking care of herself. She was doing too much for her kids. And so if her marriage became bumpy, I think she felt that it was her fault because she gained weight. So now the lesson my mother's learning is to take a little time for herself. She loved giving but it's good to have moderation in certain things. It's time for her to give to herself."

Amelia's happiness has always been linked to the happiness of her children. Even while she was in the hospital recovering from her heart attack, Amelia's thoughts remained on her kids. After she had regained consciousness, she opened up her eyes and whispered something no one understood. The kids leaned in, expecting to hear some profound words from their dying mother. Amelia said the word again and it was the title of a television show. Kim explains, "My brother John was going crazy, he said, 'She's dying, she doesn't know who we are!' " Kim's only sister, Jackie, however, remembered that their little brother Fred was supposed to make an appearance on the television show that night. Amelia wanted to make sure none of them missed their little brother's performance. Kim says with a laugh, "So you know, even on her 'deathbed' my mother was thinking about her kids. She's proud of her kids and that's her creation. And that's why we feel really lucky." ∎

Amelia Flores and her daughter, Kim Flores.

Coco's World

Lauren Velez

AND HER MOTHER,

Socorro Velez

L auren Velez has made a career out of portraying gritty, urban charac ters on popular television crime dramas such as Fox's *New York Undercover* and HBO's *Oz*. But Lauren is far more than the hard-core roles she plays on screen; she is the softhearted daughter of an amazing woman in her own right, Socorro Velez. ■ Socorro has taken her difficult childhood and transformed it into a magical world. Her shop, My Mother's Attic, is very much like the woman herself—creative, dramatic, and one-of-a-kind.

"MY MOM WAS meant to be a huge star," Lauren says, "a huge singing star! She always sings in the craziest places. We'll be on the street corner, and she'll just start singing. That's what she loves. She has a lot that she wants to give. She loves performing and I think that zapped right into me. My sisters, Lorraine and Margaret, and everyone in my family have some element of that in them. It has touched us all."

Lauren describes her mom as a highly energetic woman who loves music and loves to party. "My sisters and I would go dancing salsa Thursday nights at the Palladium," she recalls. "It would be two in the morning and my mother would not want to leave. I'd be the one to say, 'Mami, we have to go. We have to go to work tomorrow,' and she would say, 'No.' I'd say, 'Mom, we have to go. We've been here since seven o'clock!' She loves to dance, loves to be out there. She's very social. I used to be the complete opposite. I was very shy. My mom is really gregarious and loves people. I always tell her she should be the director of a cruise ship: 'Hi, I'm Coco, welcome aboard. You're in Cocoworld.' "

Lauren laughs as she recalls a time when her sister Lorraine was singing on a cruise ship and her mom came to visit. "She said by the end of the second day people were like, 'Where's Coco?' And my mom, the star, was like, 'Here I am,' her scarf blowing in the breeze in all her fabulousness! She always had a clear idea of drama and fun and how to savor every second. I'm just starting to really get it and understand it."

Socorro Velez is a larger-than-life figure who gave birth to a daughter who, naturally, would pursue a career in acting. In a sense, Coco (as she prefers to be called) has always been something of a performer herself. "People who don't know my mother, know my mother. My sisters and I always tell stories about her because she's so funny. If you made up a character like my mother, people would think it was an exaggeration. My mother needs to have her own show."

Even though their relationship was going through a difficult phase, Lauren has always looked up to Coco. "When I was young, I worshiped my mother. I thought she was infallible and was a saint. *Santa Coco!* Even when she lost her temper, I couldn't get mad at her. I was raised with the sensibility that you must have the ultimate respect for your parents. No matter what they do, you just respect and honor them. Of course, as I got older issues came up. Then therapy came up.

"There were some things that weren't so great when I was a kid and

I thought that we should discuss them. So my mom and I had to hash a few issues out. It was a really big deal for me because it went against everything I was raised to think. You don't question adults, especially your parents. But it just deepened our relationship and took us to a different place. We were always friends but I've been getting to know my mother as a woman, which is a very unique thing."

The woman that would become the infamous Coco was born in Puerto Rico. Her mother died when she was seven years old and her father brought his traumatized young daughter to live with him in New York City. Her father had remarried a woman who had three sons—one of whom became Lauren's father.

Lauren says, "Isn't that crazy? It took me years to get that straight. I would ask my mother, 'But how could Titi Miriam be your sister and Papi's sister? This is getting freaky.' So there's no blood between them; they're steps. And so my mother and father grew up together."

Lauren's mother was very young when she had her first child. Lauren's father left for the army, and when he returned, the rest of the children came all at once: one boy and seven girls. "I can't imagine having eight children. I actually don't think that you could do it today the way you could back then. But somehow my mom managed to raise eight children."

The Velez family moved from Brooklyn when Lauren was about seven years old because her parents didn't want to raise their children in an apartment. They wanted to live in a house. Coco had an idea of what she wanted for her kids, and what she wanted was something better than how she grew up. So the entire Velez clan ended up in Rockaway Beach, a community near the beach. "We grew up in a difficult household," Lauren explains. "It was an almost stereotypical Latin household in that it was loud, passionate, fiery, with music playing all the time and a lot of yelling going on."

While Lauren's childhood home may have been stereotypical, she also remembers her mother creating an idyllic environment for them to grow up in. Coco would pick up her son and daughters every day from school, give them Italian bread, salami, and cheese sandwiches, and head straight to the beach. The children would spend their afternoons playing on the beach while their mother watched them from her spot under the boardwalk. It was their own Caribbean experience in Rockaway Beach.

"It really was kind of magical. My parents would take us for strolls. My mother would take us to go see fireworks on the beach every Tuesday night. It was really enriching to have that kind of experience. It was really rich and my family was not rich. We struggled financially."

As Lauren grew older and learned more about her family, her mother was also growing and finding out more about her daughter. "When my mom came to see me perform in *The Vagina Monologues*, I was nervous. I joked for the longest time, 'God forbid my mother comes to see the show.' And when my mom came to see it, of course I froze. There we were joking around, calling it *The Toto Monologues*. But my mom was just so brilliant about it. There were things that made her uncomfortable, but we were able to have a discussion about it, a real woman-to-woman discussion. The next day I performed it again, and she said, '*Bueno*, how are you? How's your

Margaret, Lorraine, and Lauren Velez with their mother, Coco Velez.

vagina?' and I thought, 'I can't believe my mom just said that.' It was the first time we had a conversation about sex. Growing up, we didn't have the birds and the bees conversation. There was a whole conversation about sex that never happened and is only happening now. My mom will say, 'Be safe, make sure you have a condom.' These are huge, monumental things. As women, our sexuality is something that is so insanely taboo and yet, we're all about being passionate and fiery. It's so complicated.

"My mom, my sisters, and I all married very definite types of men and have very definite types of relationships. We're all very independent, pretty successful, and take care of our selves. My mom would always say, 'Listen, when your husband comes in the door, make sure he gives you his check.'

This is old school. He gives you his check, you give him money for the week, and you run the household. I told my mother that if I do that, there's an expectation that I have to stay home and my role would be the homemaker. On the other hand she'll say, 'Your career is very important and you cannot let anyone, not family, not husband, not anyone get in the way of your career.' So it's weird because times have changed so much and at warp speed. My generation has not a clue what to do right now with relationships or with jobs. I don't know what role to play and I think that it really does stem from how we were raised.

"My mother definitely practiced what she preached. She and my father were good together. My father passed away nine years ago. My dad was like a force and not an easy man at all to live with. We had a lot of hard times growing up with him. When he died, my mom didn't really change; she just became more mom. She was always such a powerful figure in my family and when she became a widow, she just got stronger. It was harder for her because this man defined her. Once he was gone, she was sort of free-floating."

Lauren explains that her mother is trying to figure out her life at sixty-plus years. "My mother tried therapy once, but Dr. Phil on *Oprah* kind of fills that slot for her. She tried therapy and I told her that she didn't have to do anything she didn't want to do. She tried it and said she didn't think it was helpful to go back, which for me was really profound. She said, 'Why stir all of that up. I'm fully aware of everything that happened. I'm fully aware of all the choices I've made. I wish I hadn't made some, some were real doozies and some were losers, but it's in the past.' "

One thing that is certain about Coco is that she doesn't live in the past and she doesn't expect her daughters to live there either. "She was always supportive, but she also supported me when I thought I wanted to be a doctor or a policewoman. She didn't push me in any direction. She's always been incredibly, incredibly supportive and she actually taught me how to conduct myself more as a professional. She would say, 'You should be in bed because you have a five A.M. call tomorrow. What are you doing out on the street?' There are certain things that she taught me about my profession. She told me once, 'I wish you would use your hands more when you act. I just want your character to be freer.' She doesn't hesitate to say, 'What happened to your hair? It's horrible.' She's hilarious but she's incredibly supportive.

"The only thing she wishes I would do is sing. It drives her crazy that I don't sing, because I used to. She says, 'I'm telling you, your fortune is gonna be in singing. Cut an album *como la* Jennifer.' My mom's a singer. I'm not joking when I say the house was full of music all the time. And she still sings. She's got a group she belongs to in New York and they do gigs all over the place. She's been singing for years, at all these different kinds of events. She tried to pursue her singing even though my father didn't want her to. So I think that's why she made sure we were in every school play.

"I would love to be a backup singer for her at one of her gigs. She probably performs once every three months. She doesn't realize how much she's actually doing. But she's actually doing her thing and living her dream. When I go see my mom's gigs, it's amazing to me that she's done it. She just trudges forward and does it. And now she'll call me or we'll call each other when she has a gig. I'll ask, 'Do you have your stuff ready?' And she'll say, "*Ay*, no.' I'll say, 'Mom, don't do that to yourself,' and she goes, 'You're right, I'm not gonna sabotage myself this time, no self-sabotage.' And we inspire each other in this way. I'll help her prepare for something and make sure she has her things, and she'll do the same thing for me. It's really kind of neat that we're both performers and can give each other advice that way that's a really nice thing to share."

But Lauren has also discovered there are many things she would prefer to keep to herself. "I have an open relationship with my mother, but I like my privacy. There are certain experiences I've had that I don't share with anybody because they're mine. There are also things that have been difficult to say to my mother and things that I've had to hash out with her that were really, really, really hard. The conversation that I would have with somebody else that might take one hour takes a week with my mother because I had to break it down in a way that would open up the discussion and have us both be comfortable in having it."

More than merely shaping Lauren and her sisters into women, Coco has shaped her very different daughters into a family. "My mom loves us all, but it's kinda neat because we're this group of women who grew up together with this woman who had us. Given what women go through, that we still speak is a testament to my mom and how she raised us. No matter what happens, my mother always says, '*Familia* is *familia*.'

"I don't know how much of that I'm gonna be able to really pass along to my family 'cause I don't know if I want to have a certain kind of energy or a certain kind of person in my life. My mother's attitude is human beings screw up. We do whacked-out stuff to each other. We hurt each other and everything comes back around. So why harbor anger?"

Not only does Coco hope to have grandchildren, she has already made a gown for her future granddaughter's christening. "My mom told me, 'I want you to have a baby.' I said, 'Right now?' and she goes, 'Yeah, I think you need to have a baby. Just have the baby and everything else is gonna fall into place.' In fact, Coco has predicted that Lauren will have two daughters of her own someday. "I really believe it. I know that my mom sees that I'm gonna have two girls. And I really want my girls to know this amazing woman. I don't want to have to show them a picture of her and say, 'That was your grandmother.' I want them to know her and feel her force.

"My mom wrote me a note in Spanish on my notepad one morning that said, 'Thank you so much for every single moment that you share with me. The beauty and the wonder and everything that you've introduced into my life, I don't know how to thank you for it, it's a joy, it's a song.' And then she wrote, 'I love you more than I could ever possibly tell you. P.S. Get a bigger notepad.'

"I have this memory of my mother that happened during an argument between my parents. They were having a really, really bad screaming argument. We were all upstairs crying, just terrified, and we could hear stuff being thrown. I just

kept thinking, 'I hope that she's okay,' and we were too scared to go downstairs to get in the middle of the fight. Finally, she came upstairs and we were all in bed just crying, just scared and crying. But she came upstairs with hot tea and she poured all of us a cup of tea. I will never forget that. We were so scared. We were lying in bed and she came in and said, 'Here, drink this, it's gonna make you feel better. Don't be afraid, this is gonna make you feel better.' She thought of us in the moment of her pain. She never let us forget we came first. She's an extraordinary woman."

Eventually, in order to escape the situation, Lauren's mother left her father. That difficult decision also meant that Coco had to leave her house. She told her children, who were already grown, that they had to stay with their father. When the time arrived that Coco wanted to return, the family convened a conference. "It was just very messy. Years later I apologized to her for that family conference. I said, 'You never know how much I regret not stopping the insanity of having a family conference. I should have just said come home, just come home.' I will never forget that moment and that's one of the most shameful moments of my life and I'm trying to work through it. And my mother said, 'You know what? The people who love you the most are the ones that are going to hurt you the most. You have to always remember that because I don't carry that around with me, I don't carry that pain, I don't carry any of it with me. All I carry with me is the love that you give me and the love that all of my children give me. The other stuff is worthless.'

"My mom is the main character in this story. This is my mom's story and we're all in it. It's her movie and it's all about her. Every single disappointment that's ours is also hers. She shares everything, every detail. And now because she has fifteen grandchildren, it really is Coco's world. If anything happens, my mom has to be on the scene. And she is really there for us in a way that's extraordinary. My mom is unlike anybody else's mom that I know. She really is all about her family.

"She's absolutely one of my best friends. But she's my mother and I like respecting her. I like the feeling of having a mother. I like the feeling that she knows more than I do because she's been around longer and I think that's great.

"I'm starting to have a really true understanding of what she means by just like going for it. My mom's a very simple woman in that way and she simply says, 'Go for it.' Go for it and do it up. Do it right. You should wear sequins to breakfast if you want to. And a boa. Go for it. Why would you not? She's like claim it, go for it, the whole thing. I'm trying to learn that."

It took years, but Lauren Velez finally realized that everything her mother ever told her was absolutely right. Lauren laughs and says, "Can you imagine? Everything she's ever said turns out to be true. It's crazy. She has very basic rules of life that apply to just about anything. Eat breakfast, eat lunch, eat dinner, don't stay out too late, moisturize, and don't be afraid to sing." ∎

Coco Velez waves her magic wand over her daughters, Margaret, Lorraine, and Lauren Velez (bottom).

And Baby Makes Three

Norma Ortiz

AND HER MOTHER,

Blanca Ortiz

A partner in the law firm Ortiz & Ortiz, Norma Ortiz joined her father's practice and introduced a whole new area of law to this successful father-and-daughter law firm. Despite the heavy demands of the legal profession, Norma has made room in her crowded world for a new resident: her brand-new baby daughter, Alena. ■ Although her daughter may share office space and a profession with her ex-husband, Blanca Ortiz plays an enormous role in her daughter's life. After retiring from a successful career as an educator, Blanca has proudly taken on the responsibility of helping to raise her granddaughter.

AND BABY MAKES THREE

WHEN THE DOCTOR first held up Norma Ortiz's newborn daughter for her to see, she was not surprised that it was a girl. Having daughters is more than a tradition in Norma's family; it is a legacy. Norma explains, "I was an only child who was primarily raised by my mother and my grandmother, so there has always been this triangle of women in the household. I always felt that if I ever had a child, I would have a daughter so I would continue that pattern." As soon as she learned that Norma was pregnant, Blanca volunteered to care for the baby while Norma worked.

Remaining true to the Ortiz women's legacy, Blanca Ortiz sold their childhood home in Queens and moved into an apartment in her daughter's apartment building in Manhattan to help raise her granddaughter. This pattern was established a generation earlier when Blanca's mother moved into the basement apartment of her house to help raise the infant Norma while Blanca pursued her career. "My grandmother lived in our house. Having a girl sort of fulfilled the fantasy that there would be another girl that would complete the four generations."

Blanca was born in Puerto Rico and immigrated to New York City when she was eleven years old. Between the ages of eleven and eighteen, Blanca lived in the States, trying to become Americanized. Acculturated to be a modern, New York young woman, Blanca decided that she wanted to return to her native Puerto Rico for college. But the Puerto Rico that she remembered from her youth was not as embracing as she expected.

Although it reawakened her cultural roots, Blanca also discovered that she no longer fit in and she would have to relearn the ways of the island. While Americans valued independence and individuality, Puerto Ricans valued the family and propriety. Blanca rediscovered a world of rules and regulations she had forgotten. She was even labeled a "bad woman" when she was seen doing the very "American" thing of smoking a cigarette in the street. But because she also picked up defiance, she smoked anyway. Eventually, Blanca set off once more for the States and decided to make a life for herself in New York City.

Norma benefited from the lessons that Blanca learned in Puerto Rico. "My mother probably gave a little bit of that rebellion to me. She told me to pursue my dreams regardless of where I was, that I have to be sure of what I want and that I should go for it. She would support me in doing things that a lot of Latin families would deter Latinas from doing. I think my mother made sure that she didn't do that to me. She didn't instill in me things that she didn't agree with." Norma's mother was able to sift through both the Puerto Rican and American cultures, instilling her daughter with both the love of family and the desire to be an independent woman.

As a young woman in New York City, Blanca decided that she would pursue her love of music. In Puerto Rico, Blanca was a soloist for her college choir and she trained to be an opera singer. However, when she won a scholarship to the prestigious Juilliard School, her dreams were crushed. Her father told her she couldn't attend. "My mother is a frustrated opera singer and a frustrated performer," says Norma, "which is very sad. It's like an artist who isn't able to paint or a dancer not being able to dance. There's nothing that brings her more joy than singing. All her life she has denied herself because she couldn't defy her father. When you meet her now, you would think she would have defied him, but I guess she didn't have what it took when she was eighteen or nineteen and people just didn't do that. I also think her father had a very strong personality in their household and she followed it."

Norma has made it a point to encourage her mother to pursue her dream of music. "She has taken classes and I've attended some performances that she's done in the last two or three years. She's sung in local clubs as a part of her classes and she sang at my wedding. But it's hard for my mother to start doing that professionally at this stage in her life. The odds that she can spin it into a career are slim."

As an only child, Norma spent many of her days with her grandmother. Unlike her very driven mother, her grandmother only boasted a sixth-grade education and couldn't speak English well. Norma has very fond memories of this woman and those times. "My grandmother was the source of unconditional love for me. I could say that about my parents to a lesser extent, but they always pushed me to achieve. It was very important to both of my parents that my grades were very high, but my grandmother was always gentle, and not as complicated as my parents were. She was always there for me no matter what. My parents were not always around, but my grandmother was always there. I would run to her if I had an argument with my mother or I got scolded. What I remember is the warmth and the kindness. That's not to say that my parents were not warm or kind, but not to the extent that my grandmother was."

Norma Ortiz and her mother, Blanca Ortiz.

While Norma's grandmother was taking care of her, Norma's mother took care of business. "My mother wasn't always a teacher, but she was always in education. She was a teacher for a few years and then she went straight to the central board of education where she was the director of bilingual education. In the seventies, she was at the forefront of pushing bilingual education in New York City. She was an advocate and somewhat of an activist in the education arena at that time. I remember her going away to conferences in South America.

"My mother has a very distinct and strong personality, so I remember her being more outgoing and more of a go-getter than other mothers that I was exposed to. From the time when I was seven to eleven years old, my mother had a television show and I would go with her to the tapings on Saturday mornings. She would teach English to Spanish speakers on a local TV station. I have this image of my mother with her whole face filling the television screen, articulating and teaching English. That made a big impression on me."

Because of her background and passion for education, Blanca made certain that her daughter benefited from her knowledge. "She spent a lot of time teaching me how to read with flash cards. By the time I was in pre-k or kindergarten, I was reading and that's why I ended up going to private school. I had problems at public schools, and I remember being brought into the principal's office with my mother. They told her I was bored, and that they should either skip me to a higher grade or take me out of the school. So they put me in private school because in those days they thought skipping was a bad thing for children.

"My mother put a huge emphasis on schoolwork. I know that that didn't come from my grandmother or my father, because after my parents divorced he was not around that much except on weekends. So I know that my mother was instrumental."

Thinking of her relationship with her mother, Norma imagines what type of relationship she'll have with her baby daughter. "My perception is that girls stay closer to the home and tend to stay more connected to their mother. It's a stereotype that's not always true, but I've thought that a daughter would stay closer to home and stay involved more than a son."

Norma says that she was raised by an intelligent, independent, and professional mother who taught her there were no limitations as to what she could achieve as a woman. Perhaps because Blanca spent her life fighting the stereotypes of what was expected of a Latina, Norma did not have to. "When I was growing up, there wasn't a lot of distinction made in the family between girls and boys, and I think that that has been an advantage to me especially professionally. So I don't think that I will raise my daughter differently than if she were a son. The only place I could see a difference is in talking to her about what to accept in romantic relationships. But professionally, athletically, culturally, or educationally, I would treat my daughter the same as a boy. I would not teach her that there are limitations for her, because I wasn't taught that there were. My mother taught me that I could do whatever I wanted to do.

"Growing up I was encouraged to pursue whatever I was interested in and whatever made me happy. My mother encouraged me to have boyfriends, to find relationships that make me happy, and to find friends that were positive for me. And if I wanted to go scuba diving and that's what I loved to do, my mother wouldn't question it. That was her primary goal and I think that she really helped develop my sense of self. My mother and my father never stopped me from doing anything I was interested in. Their primary concern was my happiness, so if my happiness involved doing something a little risky, they supported that."

One of the things that her mother had to grin and bear was Norma's love of animals. "It's a very primitive love for me and my mother never encouraged it. I've always had dogs and although my mother complained the whole way, she never stopped me from having the animals. My father was not supportive of my pets either; actually, he doesn't even like animals.

"I've always been obsessed by nature and animals. I remember my parents bought me a natural museum book with four hundred pages and I went through all the species of animals and plants and bugs. That book was my bible and I would take it into the forest by myself and I would identify the plants and classify the animals, I was always obsessed with nature and animals."

And as often happens in families, the many, many dogs that Norma brought home quickly became the responsibility of her mother and her grandmother. They had little choice. Later, in college, Norma took out a student loan to buy her first parrot.

"I thought I was going to be a marine biologist, it's really what I wanted to do. I wanted to be a naturalist and I think my pets are a reflection of that part of me. I still hope that I'm financially secure enough at some point in my life to have a wildlife rehabilitation sanctuary, and to actually do something hands-on. It's an instinctual love of life."

Norma's love of life hasn't stopped with the more pedestrian dogs and parrots. The king of her jungle is an iguana that stretches just under five feet long. Norma smiles but becomes defensive: "No one has a relationship with my iguana except me. I have three parrots and the iguana and every morning I have to make food for them. The cleaning and maintenance is tough. It probably takes at least forty minutes a day, which in our lives is a lot of time. Honestly, if I had to do it again, I would not have the animals because it's not conducive to living in an apartment in Manhattan. I love them but it's very difficult. It's probably another example of trying to maintain my own identity, because no one has supported me in this. I've been threatened and insulted and harassed and I can't tell you how much opposition I've had to maintaining the animals and I still keep them."

When Norma first announced her pregnancy, her husband and her mother assumed that the iguana would have to find a home elsewhere once the baby arrived. They were mistaken. Norma insisted that the reptile and baby human could live under the same roof. Coincidentally, the iguana removed itself from the picture by dying a few short weeks after the baby's arrival. Norma was heartbroken but her daughter and her career didn't leave her with much time to grieve.

Far from the world of nature preserves and exotic animals, Norma's path took her to an unlikely career in law. "My father told me, 'You are going to go to law school.' If I would tell him I wanted to do something else, he wasn't as supportive." Norma's dad wanted her to become a lawyer so that she could work with him and inherit his law practice. If life under two very strong-willed parents has been difficult at times, it has ultimately proved to be very rewarding.

"I think that my mother and my father have paved the way for me in a lot of ways," Norma states. "I have less to prove because my parents proved a lot before me. I am more comfortable with where I am and where I have been. Both of my parents are extremely opinionated and very controlling. My mother has a strong personality and character that could be overwhelming. You have to fight to keep your own voice and that's what I did."

When Norma was ten years old, her parents divorced, and unlike many children of divorce, she was able to analyze what happened. While she wanted her parents to stay together, she realized why it had to happen. "They fought a lot, so I understood. My mother was unhappy in the marriage and that was clear to me.

"Their marriage was strained for as long as I could remember. My father was politically and civically very active, so he wouldn't come home until nine, ten, eleven, one o'clock in the morning. I don't have memories of my father during the week sitting down and eating dinner with us. My memories of him are all from the weekends. On weekends we would go to his country house upstate, and that's where I have my nuclear-family memories."

After her parents' divorce, Norma's father not only didn't disappear but he moved only a block away from his ex-wife and daughter. Blanca made it a point to make sure that her daughter had a relationship with her father. "I went from house to house. My father was such a strong influence in my life that even if my mother would have tried to keep him out, she couldn't have done that because I was always very close to him."

As close as she is to her father, Norma is especially close to her mother. "I can tell my mother whatever is on my mind, up to a point. It's probably one of the reasons why my

Norma Ortiz, pregnant with her daughter, Alena, is embraced by her mother, Blanca Ortiz.

mother lives upstairs from me now. My husband was concerned initially but now he agrees that she should be there. My mother has always respected my privacy and my space. She's very sensitive to intruding too much in my life. She would rather err on the side of not butting in as opposed to butting in. So whenever she crosses the line or does something I'm not comfortable with, I tell her and she backs off. I think that has enabled us to be as close as we are and to spend as much time as we do together because we have that line of communication."

With grandmother, mother, and daughter living under the same roof, it appears that things have traveled full circle. Blanca wants to help raise her granddaughter just as her mother helped raise her daughter. And Norma couldn't be happier.

"I'm very grateful. I consider myself very lucky, but I'm not surprised: my mother's always wanted this. If it were up to my mother, she would have had more children. If it were up to my mother, she would have remarried. If it were up to my mother, she would have been surrounded by a lot of people. But that's just not how her life worked out.

"Alena is like pure joy to my mother and I thought it would be that way. And to be honest, there's a little part of me that wanted a baby for my mother. I always wanted to have a child, so it was ninety-nine percent me, but there's a little one percent there where I knew a baby would bring a lot of joy to my mother. So Alena's here in part because of my mother or for my mother. My mother's in this point in life where she has the time to do this. I'm happy, but I sort of knew it would be like this." ∎

A Whole Other World

Esmeralda Santiago

AND HER MOTHER,

Ramona Santiago

Esmeralda Santiago has taken her often painful experiences of growing up in Puerto Rico and New York and transformed them into the critically acclaimed memoirs *When I Was Puerto Rican* and *Almost a Woman.* After attending Performing Arts High School, Esmeralda graduated with highest honors from Harvard University and received a master's degree from Sarah Lawrence College. ■ Esmeralda is the daughter of Ramona Santiago, an adventurous woman who raised eleven kids in an alien place far from her family and home. The lessons Ramona taught her daughter, intentional and unintentional, helped Esmeralda realize that she had to seek her own adventure beyond her mother's home.

Esmeralda Santiago was thirteen years old when she first left Puerto Rico for the United States. For her mother, Ramona, Brooklyn was a terrifying world. Her youngest son needed medical care and it seemed like no one spoke Spanish. "For the first few months Mami took me everywhere with her, even though I didn't speak any more English than she did. She would never go alone. I felt completely responsible. Like I had to take care of her. And I made sure I did."

Esmeralda and her family soon discovered that there was a vast difference between the world they had abandoned and the world they adopted, a difference that went far beyond mere language. "My mother wanted me to be a good girl. But the difference between a good thirteen-year-old girl in Puerto Rico and thirteen-year-old girls in Brooklyn was enormous and I wanted to be like the girls in Brooklyn. The Brooklyn girls wore the short skirts, the makeup, the hairdos. I wanted all those things and she would not allow it. She wouldn't even let me wear a bra. I remember that my boobies were beginning to bounce around when I was in gym, and the boys teased me. My mother sewed bras in the garment district, so I remember saying, 'Mami, I need a bra.' And she said, 'No. Tu estas muy nena, besides you don't have anything to hold up.' So her cousin, brought me a couple of bras the next time she came over. But she made the mistake of making them black. My mother said, 'Absolutely not! You can't wear black bras. That's for *putas*.' "

If Ramona appeared old-fashioned to her daughter, she also appeared to be fearless. Esmeralda realized that her mother wasn't the helpless woman she thought she was. "My mother is very adventurous. Her life has definitely been an amazing adventure. When she came to the U.S., she was twenty-nine and already had seven children. She left her husband, the house they owned, and everyone she knew to come to New York without knowing the language, and we didn't go back. If she had money, she probably would be traveling all over the world. To do what she did took a lot of courage and vision and, yes, maybe it took some thought, although I don't believe she thought it all the way through."

Growing up, Esmeralda has always seen herself as her mother's protector. Like other children of immigrants, she became her mother's unofficial translator and guide. It was a role that has followed her into adulthood. "I remember being a little kid and telling my mother, 'Mami, when I grow up and I'm rich, I'm going to buy you a house.' And I haven't done that. So I feel like I owe her a house.

"Our lives were one rented place

after another ever since I can remember. And even the place where she lives now near Orlando, Florida, is a trailer, so she's still renting the space that she lives in. In fact, something very scary happened and I don't think she knows the implications of it. She said she received a letter that said the trailer park had been sold. I said, 'What do you mean it's been sold?' And she said it's under new management and they're just going to raise her rent a little bit. I thought to myself these people could make the trailer park the next Wal-Mart. I'm afraid that in the next few months I'm going to get a tearful call from her saying, 'What am I supposed to do? I can't move this trailer.' The trailer is thirty years old. She's probably going to be faced with yet another move and basically have to set up another home.

"The fact that she lives in a trailer is probably harder for me than for her because I know that she wants a nice house. She put tiles all over her trailer. She has spent so much money tiling that thing. I think she's trying to re-create the homes in Puerto Rico that she always wanted to have. I've definitely put the responsibility to get her a house on myself. She's never mentioned it. I feel like she sacrificed a lot for her eleven kids. She gave up a lot, most significantly her youth. And she never had very much. Everything that she has ever had she spent on her children and on making our home a place that would be good for everybody. That meant we all had to make compromises because we always have our own idea of what our home should be like."

And Ramona's homes have always been full of people she can entertain. "I know that's what she wants: a place where her eleven kids and grandkids can come over and feel comfortable staying and not have to worry whether there are enough rooms. As her children became older and moved away and had their own families, Mami has been having less and less opportunity to entertain and she misses it."

Because of the physical distance between them, Ramona's welfare has increasingly become an issue, not only to Esmeralda but to her brothers and sisters as well. "A couple of years ago,

Ramona Santiago with her granddaughter, Ila Cantor, and her daughter, Esmeralda Santiago.

my sister Edna bought Mami a condo in New Windsor, New York, which is where Edna lives. Mami didn't like it there but she felt *obligada*. The condo was not in a neighborhood. The first week she lived there, she went to the local hospital to see if she could volunteer. They told her, 'Oh, we only take high school students.' Mami said, 'I can't even give away my time!' She was really depressed. She knew going in that she wasn't going to like New Windsor because it's cold and she hates winter. She moved to a community where she knew no one. She's used to being near everything and this was in the country. She knew all those things and yet she said *'no me atrevia decircle a ella que no,'* she just didn't want to disappoint my sister. So she was unhappy the year that she spent in New York, all because she was trying to make Edna happy. She ended up returning to Florida and feeling like she disappointed her daughter. Edna was annoyed with her, and it became *un bochinche* [gossip], and I said I'm staying out of it. But I can't stay out of it.

"If Mami had only told Edna that what she really wanted was a condo in Kissimmee, Florida, it would've saved Edna tens of thousands of dollars. It would've saved Mami thousands of dollars and a year of incredible anguish, illness, emotional ups and downs, and depression.

"Mami loves where she is in Florida, mostly because of her job. She works at a day-care center for people with Alzheimer's disease. Her coworkers value her. She's so attached to the clients that when she lived in New York for a year, all she kept saying to us was, *'Me hacen falta los viejitos.'* [I miss my little old people.] She's been a caretaker all her life and she found this place, and she loves taking care of people who need her and that brings meaning to her life.

"She would love to have a house, but she wants it in Kissimmee. She wants it there so that she can stay close to where she's making a real contribution to people's lives in the most unselfish, generous way you can imagine. She is genuine in her desire to help and to be of service. She's been that way her entire life. Mami raised her children and then she raised five or six of her husband's children after his wife died. She wouldn't let her mother go to some nursing home, so Tata lived with her until she died in her arms. Mami stayed with her and nursed her through every illness. She has always been like that."

Unlike the life Ramona remembered as a child in Puerto Rico, the children in contemporary American families tend to leave the nest. This conflict remains an ongoing problem that Latina immigrants have to deal with—balancing the powerful expectation that daughters have to be the family caretakers with the daughter's own dreams and desires. And like other American families, Esmeralda and her siblings struggle with their responsibility to their mother. "It's really complicated in our family because there are eleven of us and the brothers and the sisters have different responsibilities. We all help Mami in different ways. There are six sisters and five brothers, so every time there's a move, it's the brothers, grandsons, and brothers-in-law who move her. And believe me, it's a job to move her! I'm glad I don't have that job because it happens frequently. They also try to make sure that things function in her new place. The sisters contribute money, companionship, and their spouses and children. I give her an allowance every month and whenever there's a big expense, she calls me. But if each of us gave a hundred dollars a month, she would have a thousand dollars a month to live on, which is more than enough for her. But nobody can commit to that, and it's like my mother-in-law says, 'One mother can take care of eleven children, but eleven children can't take care of one mother.' And it's true, and it's our shame.

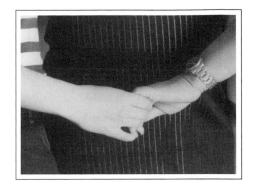

"Soon after we arrived in the U.S., Mami started to become less mythical to me. The worst thing that ever happened to me, in terms of my relationship with her, was when I realized she couldn't take care of me. When I went to the welfare office and she told them she didn't have food and she needed money for rent because we might get evicted, it was absolutely terrifying. It would be terrifying to any kid, never mind one who was struggling with all the other things that I was struggling with, like language and culture and adjusting to life in Brooklyn. And I think that that's when I began to make decisions about myself. I reached the point where I began to understand that I had to start making decisions that were different from hers. I realized I couldn't do everything she told me because, as I could see, it was not working for her."

Esmeralda reached the first of many major turning points in her life when she realized that her life would not be her mother's. As frightening as that was, it was also surprisingly liberating. "I still have very strong memories of the places where I made actual intellectual decisions about why my life had to be different from hers or in what way it had to be different from hers. When Mami was younger, she was much more hysterical, in the sense of being much more emotional. She had a lot more to deal with, of course, but I began to cultivate the idea of not letting anything throw me.

"In many ways, she's the reason that I write. I've gone through all the stages that every child goes through with their parents. I've gone through total adoration, to realizing that they aren't godlike, to being annoyed, to 'I can't stand my parents and I'm never going back there,' to beginning to understand who they are and completely forgiving all the things and asking forgiveness, then finally having a real adult relationship with them. My work tries to track that process because I am aware of having gone through all those stages. When you are going through them, however, you are not as aware.

"When I began to write *When I Was Puerto Rican*, my relationship with my parents was still ambivalent. I hadn't come to terms with what my relationship was. I had guilt if I didn't call and I had the annoyance if I did call. It would get in the way of my private life, but I just had to go through all those things before I started to write the book."

Selling over sixteen thousand copies in hardcover, *When I Was Puerto Rican* made a grand entrance onto the literary stage. It was hailed by both critics and audiences as audaciously candid and revealing. More than a story about growing up in rural Toa Baja and urban Brooklyn, the memoir was an intimate portrait of a young Latina stepping outside of the role assigned to her and examining not only her life but the lives of her parents as well.

"I said, 'I'm going to write what I remember. I'm not going to judge it. I'm just going to write it the way I remember it.' I had to think hard about my relationship with my parents. How did I feel about them? What is it like to be these people's child? And it was at that point that I made the literary decision to write the book chronologically from the perspective of the child. I remember sitting down at my desk and saying, 'What is the first thing I remember? What was it like? Did I love my mom? Did I love my dad?' I constantly asked myself questions about them and that's where the book came from. And the picture emerges of this very strong woman and this girl who tries to both please her and get away from her.

"I really was in love with my dad. I was a disappointment to my mom. I was a disappointment for a long time because I wasn't my father's boy and I wasn't my mother's little rosy-cheek, bow-wearing, frilly girl. I never was that and I never will be. As part of our relationship, I had to come to terms with the fact that I was not the daughter that Mami expected. Our mothers really want little dolls and I was never the little doll.

"The way she tells it, when I was little, I was a screamer.

I was a terrible baby and I was always hyper. She was seventeen when she had me, so I was not an easy child for a teenager to deal with. Then after me comes Delsa, who looks like a little doll. She was premature, so she was tiny and cute and really pretty and had the Shirley Temple ringlets and the whole works. For the longest time, I remember growing up thinking Delsa is the pretty one and I'm the troublemaker. I was a good kid, but I was the one who, if Mami heard somebody crying, she would know I'd caused it. I was always testing her limits.

"The big breakthrough for me was to say I'm going to forgive my parents for all the things that hurt me and disappointed me and made me angry. I'm going to forgive them because I realize that they did the best they could. There probably are parents who are evil and they probably do evil things just because they are evil people, but I would say the vast majority of mothers and fathers do the best they can with what they have. I think my mom did the best she could with what she had and she didn't have much, so my sisters and brothers got as much as you can possibly get from somebody.

"When I started going to Performing Arts High School, I realized that there was a whole other world that was not centered around my family, or around my neighborhood, or around the people I knew. There was a whole other culture that I had access to that nobody I knew in that community had interest in. They wouldn't leave the neighborhood. I know people who have never left *el barrio* and I'm speaking literally. I had aunts that took pride in the fact that they had never taken the subway across the East River into Manhattan. So when I started going out and realized there was this whole other world, I realized how narrow my family's world was. For them it was fine, and it worked a long time for my sisters and brothers although things have changed as they've matured. And it worked for years for my mother. But it didn't work for me. I needed a bigger world right away."

Esmeralda realized as an adolescent that what she wanted and needed wasn't going to be found in her Brooklyn neighborhood. "I was looking for a sense of myself that was self-defined, that wasn't defined by culture or by family or by other people. It was an intellectual decision, not an emotional decision. I loved my family and I wished I could stay with them, but the things that I needed were not there and I thought I'd never get them there. Mami wanted to protect me, but she was keeping me from the experiences that I so desperately wanted. And the experience that I most wanted was that of being for myself, by myself."

Esmeralda recalls when, as a young woman, she climbed to the top of the Empire State Building and looked out at that famous vista for the first time. "I wanted to know what was beyond the horizon. I knew that the United States was vast. I knew that the horizon I saw didn't begin to show how big this country was and I wanted to see it. I wanted to expand my mind, expand my intellect, learn things, and be open to other worlds of experience. I could've had it within the embrace of my family without leaving them, but not when I needed it. Mami had ten other children and I was the oldest one. Part of my wanting to get away was because I knew what Mami wanted for me and my sisters and brothers and I didn't want to set a bad example. I didn't want them to

see me stumble. I didn't want to do anything that would bring them shame or embarrassment. But I also didn't want to do things that would bring me shame or embarrassment. And for me to not pursue my ambition would have been shameful.

"To me, Mami has always represented unbridled passion. She represents emotion at a very raw level that is not tempered by much thought. She's impetuous. I think that almost all of her big decisions have come from an emotional place. I tend to be intuitive, but I think things through more and I'm clearer about what I want, but I also worry more about the consequences of my actions.

"The most confusing thing for me as an adolescent was her 'Do as I say and not as I do' thing. Sex is a big part of mother-daughter misunderstandings in our culture. I mean, sex is going to come up. It's going to happen whether you are straight, gay, celibate, or whatever. It is an issue. And in my case, my mother lived with five different men so far. Yet her expectation was that we were supposed to get married in the church and not have sex before marriage. We never went to church, but we were supposed to get married in the church, *con el velo, el traje blanco*, the whole business. But she never did it. She would meet a man and they knew each other for a few months. They would go to a couple of dances and then one day, he would be there the next morning. But we couldn't do that. I never saw my mother as a hypocrite. I always thought she was straight with us and it's not like she pretended these men weren't there. She's always been open. So why was it that there was this double standard? It finally occurred to me that she really felt like it was too late for her, but it was not too late for me or my sisters. She still had dreams for us.

"When I was growing up I could not get a birth control pill unless Mami signed a paper. I think you had to be twenty-one or something like that. So I just didn't have sex. It was simple for me. Now you talk to a seventeen-year-old girl and she's like, 'Oh, but my boyfriend will leave me.' My attitude was he could leave anyway. From an early age, I built a strong sense of myself that did not necessarily include being defined by my romantic relationships. Of course when I did get into a relationship, when I was twenty-one, I went completely counter to all that.

"I didn't tell Mami I was leaving with this guy. I left her a letter. She had no idea I'd been seeing him and I couldn't tell her because I didn't know how to tell her. I didn't want to hurt her, but I also didn't want to ask permission. This whole thing happened after I had been engaged to another man and I got cold feet. I was twenty. I had the dress and the veil and the church all lined up. It was a very big disappointment for Mami when I didn't get married. I knew that I couldn't tell her about the other man because I was afraid that she wouldn't let me go even though I was twenty-one. If I insisted on going, it would've been worse. It was a very difficult decision because I knew I was leaving for good. I knew that I could never come back. My pride and her pride wouldn't allow it."

Esmeralda left her mother and her family for seven long years even though she missed her mother and often felt lonely. Despite the very different course her life took from her mother's, she found that she wanted to establish contact again. "I hadn't seen them for about eight years. They returned to Puerto Rico and I was in the U.S. I was almost afraid to go see them because *no me querí enmarañar* in their lives. My memory of my family's life was of one crisis after another, without a breather. That was the way it was and I think it is still that way for some of my siblings. I didn't want that. I don't want every single moment to be an emergency. I wanted to be more balanced.

Reestablishing contact with her mother told Esmeralda both that she missed her mother and that they were simultaneously alike and different. "We are similar, but I've taken her traits one step further. Unfortunately for me, I was taking steps away from my culture because our culture is a communal culture. I still know so many Latinas who don't go anywhere alone. I have Latina friends who are successful business executives who would not go to a movie by themselves. They won't do it. You have to be *con alguien*. If that's a Latina trait or, let's say, a Puerto Rican trait, then I'm not very Puerto Rican that way because there is nothing I enjoy more than to just be by myself. I go up to Maine for two or three months *solita tranquila* and I'm happy. My dad was like that and my mother was always criticizing him because he liked to be alone. So I got something from both of them: her spirit of adventure and his—I guess you'd call it a comfort with yourself.

"One of the first things I decided when I left home was to stop living for other people. That was what really separated me from my family at that point because I became selfish. I was no longer worried about what people thought. I still don't care. They don't live with me and they don't live inside my head, so it doesn't matter what the neighbors or cousins or aunts think. It's not important to me, but it's very important in our community and it was important to my mother and it's still important to the family."

Eventually, Esmeralda created a family of her own and suddenly had the opportunity to create her own traditions and sense of what a mother should be. Although she was the oldest of her mother's children, she was one of the last to be married. "I didn't get married until I was thirty. I wasn't going to get pregnant when I was a teenager and I wasn't going to have kids until I felt like I was settled, whatever that meant for me at the time. I wasn't going to tie myself down to a man. I had boyfriends and I dated and I had a good time, but there was no way that I was going to do what Mami did in terms of constantly giving her heart to men who broke it. Men who would abandon her, or betray her, or have children, then abandon them. I just couldn't do that. I said, 'You know if that means *que me quedo jamona me quedo jamona*, that's it.'

"I also had children late. I was thirty-two when Lucas was born and I was thirty-six when Ila was born. It was then that I began to see the wisdom of what my mother did and the way she did it. And not just the wisdom, but the incredible effort and her sense of adventure and all the things I didn't appreciate or value when I was younger.

"There are moments where I kind of stop myself and say, 'I am doing something I wish my mother hadn't done to me.' Ila is very good at reminding me when I behave in a way that's much more primal than what she's used to and then we talk about it. We have a good relationship. I've had conversations with my daughter that I never had with my mother and don't know if I'll ever have with my mother.

My daughter is seventeen and we have a very different relationship from the one I had with Mami. You know there is this whole concept of *respeto* in our culture and I think what happens is that *respeto* gets extended to places where, when something becomes uncomfortable to talk about, then it becomes *falta de respeto*. We don't talk about things that we have to talk about because of that *falta de respeto* issue, which usually goes in one direction because the younger person is *faltándole respeto* to the older one. It's very rarely used the other way because your mother will feel like she can comment about anything, but you can't do it the other way. That's one of the things that is different in my relationship with my daughter. There is that mutual respect where I try hard to be respectful of her as an individual.

"There are very beautiful values in our culture, but if they are misused or abused, they end up being a disadvantage to us rather than an advantage. We can turn it into an advantage if *respeto* goes both ways, but most of the time *respeto* goes upwards. Very rarely in our culture does it go downward.

"I don't think I am a perfect parent, but I try to be conscious of those things because I know what was missing in my relationship with my mother. I wished I had a mother who went into my room and just hugged me. Yesterday I came down to my daughter's room and I just hugged her and kissed her. She was totally shocked and said, 'What was that for?' I said, 'Well, I haven't seen you in eight hours and I wanted to hug you and kiss you.' Then she had this expression on her face that was so wonderful that, even though I felt kind of silly, I knew that I had done the right thing. I didn't have that kind of relationship with Mami. She didn't have time, and to her *respeto* meant that she couldn't be too affectionate. If you are too affectionate *te pueden faltar el respeto.*"

Esmeralda has found that she can take lessons learned from her mother and combine them with the hard lessons she's learned from her own life to create a relationship that works for both her and her daughter. "It's terrifying to have an open relationship with your daughter. It's scary because they can ask you anything. It's scary to be a mother. You don't really want to know some things. You don't necessarily want to talk about some things. You don't necessarily want to answer all their questions. You don't even want to know what's on their minds sometimes.

"I know there's going to come a time when my daughter will have to make a decision that means I'm going to lose her. Right now, I still have a part of her. She's seventeen, so there's a part of her that still belongs to me, but it's coming up very soon, whether she chooses to go to college, or the guy she chooses to date, or whatever. I mean I don't know what it will be, but in every parent's life that moment arrives and should arrive.

"Mothers are human beings and they have the exact feelings, worries, and concerns that everyone does. It's just that they are worrying for themselves and for us. We are only worried about ourselves until we have children and then we worry about ourselves, our children, and about our mothers."

Regardless of how battered their relationship has been over the years, the connection between Ramona, Esmeralda, and Ila stands firm. "Ila and my mother have a very sweet relationship. Ila loves her so purely, so completely. I wish I had that love for my grandmother. When I see Mami and Ila, it's bittersweet. Ila is not a touchy-feely person, but my mother will touch her and hug her and Ila just completely gives herself to her. That's one thing they say about grandchildren, they don't have the baggage that your children have, so there is that pure relationship that you can't have with your own kids. A grandchild also doesn't have the history that the child does.

"I now have an adult relationship with Mami. It's not the same as I have with my girlfriends and I don't want it to be that way. I want a mother. The only thing I wish that I could do for her is to get her the house that I promised her. I feel like she deserves it. She should have it. And I will consider my life a success if I could give it to her." ∎

Between Two Worlds

Miriam Weintraub

AND HER MOTHER,

Alma Weintraub

Winner of the prestigious Peabody, Emmy, and RFK Memorial Awards, Miriam Weintraub has soared to the top in the world of television journalism. Miriam has served as producer on the highly rated and highly regarded *60 Minutes* and *60 Minutes II*. ■ Although her job takes her to the far corners of the globe, Miriam always finds her way back to the Cuban Jewish community in Miami that she was raised in. While her mother's life couldn't appear to be more different, Alma Weintraub is the cultural backbone to her very driven daughter.

WHEN MIRIAM WEINTRAUB called her mother to let her know she was pregnant, she asked if she wanted her future grandchild to call her Bubbie or Abuelita. It was a significant and very telling question. *Bubbie* is the Yiddish translation, and *Abuelita* is the Spanish, for "grandmother." Her mother, Alma, answered, *"Abuelita. Estas jugando!"* [You're kidding!]

"My mother speaks Spanish and English, and she has a heavy Cuban accent she has never been able to get rid of." Miriam explains, "She went to college in Miami to lose her accent. But because all of her teachers were Cubans, she didn't lose her accent at all.

"She was born in Havana, Cuba, in 1941. She left when she was nineteen, in 1960. Her parents were born in Poland and Lithuania. Both sets of my grandparents are Eastern European Jews who went to Cuba in the twenties. They left Poland because of persecution. They arrived in Havana on the same boat, basically penniless.

"My grandparents wanted to get into the United States but there was a quota against Eastern Europeans entering the U.S. at that time. So what a lot of people did was go to Cuba and then apply to get into the U.S. from there. When my grandparents got to Cuba, the law changed and it no longer mattered where you applied from; it mattered where you were born. So they stayed in Cuba. They developed a life, picked up the culture, learned the language and loved it."

Jewish immigrants played significant roles in the political and economic life of Cuba and the Cuban government welcomed them, supporting the establishment of the Zionist organization and the Centro Israelita de Cuba. In the 1920s, there was a dramatic increase in Jewish immigration from Europe. By the 1950s, there were over twelve thousand Jews who were well established and integrated in Cuba. When the new Communist government took control of Cuba in 1960, the Cuban Jews were among the many other Cubans who were forced to flee their homeland.

"The Jews in Cuba lived a sort of self-imposed ghetto life," Miriam explains. "My mother went to a Jewish school where they taught her Yiddish and Spanish. But she wasn't Orthodox Jewish; she was just culturally Jewish. I mean she ate ham. She was Cuban. She looked like a Cuban girl but I don't think that they mixed much with other people. My mother still has friends from Cuba and there are a few who are Catholic, but most of her friends are Jews. They gravitated towards each other in Cuba and now that they live in the United States, all her friends are Cuban Jews. We call them Jewbans. My mom loved Cuba. It's still her country and, just like all the other Cubans, they feel very emotional about their home."

While mother and daughter both describe themselves as Cuban-American Jews and share a culture, there is another culture that separates the two women. Miriam says, "My mother and I are different in that I'm educated—overeducated. Not that my mother is not smart, but she wasn't formally educated, so that was never important to her. She probably wonders if she overeducated me in a way, because if I hadn't gone to college, I would be home with two kids, living three blocks from mommy, going there for food. My older brother still goes there to have his laundry done."

Miriam doesn't remember her mother working while she was growing up. "My memory was that she was always home. My mother believes in those unwritten rules that women are supposed to be good mothers and wives. She thinks a college education helps you, but didn't necessarily think I needed to go to an Ivy League school. She would have been just as happy, and maybe happier, if I had been the kind of person who wanted to go to the University of Miami, or the University of Florida, and be close to home." Despite a difference in priorities, Miriam says that her mom has always supported her as she pursued the life she created for herself. "She may not have been the person who made me take my SATs because it wasn't her thing, but she never stopped me from doing what I felt I had to do.

"I had some inner drive that said I was not only going to be in student council; I was going to be president of my school. I was and she supported it. I wasn't just going to go to a good school; I was going to go to the best school I could. I was going to go to graduate school. I can't say that any of that was what my mother would have dreamt of for me. She probably would have preferred that I was more of a normal Cuban daughter like some of her friends have, the kind that got married at twenty-two. They are women who work with their husbands and have three kids. All of my mother's friends

Alma Weintraub and her daughter, Miriam Weintraub, in Miami, Florida.

have multiple grandchildren, three, four, and five. Some of them are teenagers now because people of my generation of Cuban-Americans got married young. They finished high school; maybe they went to the University of Miami or some of the other Miami schools. They got married, had their kids, and they probably worked as a receptionist in their husband's dentist's office or with their husband in real estate. My mother knew early on that that was just not me. I was different. I wanted more and I need more."

Miriam describes herself as the girl who wore jeans and a T-shirt while her mom wore high heels even to go to the movies. "I would tell her, 'Put some sneakers on, it's more comfortable.' And my mother would say, 'Oh no, they're not comfortable for me. *Yo me caigo en sneakers*' [I fall in sneakers]. Because she's getting older, she's wearing a little smaller heel, but she's always made up. My mother never leaves the house without makeup. She never leaves the house without her hair looking like it just came from the beauty parlor. She's really Miami when it comes to that. It's what makes her happy."

No matter how different these two women may appear, the language, life, and love that they share is far greater than anything that could ever separate them.

"When I go down to Miami, I tell my mom, 'Let's go get our nails done.' We shop. In Miami that's a mother-daughter thing. I do those Miami things and I can be the Miami person. We also like to travel together. My mother loves Cuban music and we went to Cuba together, and last year we went to Guatemala together. Guatemala is not a place that any of her friends would go to because it's dangerous. But she wanted to go, so I said, 'Let's go.'

"When we were in Guatemala, I realized we're the same person. Not in the way we dress or what we look like, but inside we're the same person. In Guatemala and in Cuba, there wasn't a person that we didn't talk to—from the person who cleaned your room to the person who drove your taxi, to the women selling chocolate on the side of the road. We talk to everybody and we want to hear their stories. I think that's why I'm good at my job because I listen to everybody's story. I listen to people and I realized on the streets of Guatemala that I must have learned it from her. We talked to everybody together and, because we both speak Spanish, people feel comfortable with us. The people we met invited us to their homes. So I think that we are different but we're very much alike."

Miriam not only credits her mother for giving her an interest in journalism, but she says her career belongs to Alma as well. A table in Alma's home, shows just how proud she is of Miriam. "She has all the baby pictures of her friends' and relatives' grandchildren. But on that same table, she has the first thing I produced. It has my credit from *60 Minutes* that says 'Produced by Miriam Weintraub.' I didn't bring her a grandchild, but I brought her that.

"I think she's learned that this is me. More than anything she's wanted a grandchild, but ten years ago she realized, "I'm not getting grandchildren any time soon," and she started volunteering in a shelter for abused and neglected kids because she had all this love to give.

"For somebody with a very fulfilled life, this is the one place where she was not fulfilled. None of her children got married until recently. She didn't talk about it. She never made us feel bad. When I found out I was pregnant, my husband Steve didn't want me to tell her until we went to the doctor. I spoke to her right after we took the first test. After I hung up I said, 'She knows.' And he said, 'What do you mean?' I told him she always knows. When I was in college she would call me and know that I had had a bad day. If a boy broke up with me, she didn't even know I was dating somebody but she just would have a feeling. I used to tell her she was a witch, but she says it's just this connection I think all mothers and daughters probably have. She calls it *mamitis*.

"So the day that I had just taken the pregnancy test she called and said, '*Yo quiero verte* [I want to see you]. I'm gonna come to Washington. *Tengo mamitis;* during the last few days I have *mamitis*.' I said, 'All right, whatever. Gotta go.' I hung up and I told Steve, 'She knows.' "

Unfortunately, shortly after this interview was completed, Miriam learned that because of complications in her pregnancy, she had lost the baby. On the day it happened, her mother was flying back from a vacation in Chile. For almost twenty-four hours, Miriam couldn't reach her mother and tell her the sad news. "At first I had imagined that she would know—in some strange, sixth sense *mamitis* way, that she'd figured it out from thousands of miles away. This time she hadn't. So when I broke the news to her I cried for the first time. I don't think it was real to me until I shared the news with her."

A few months later, Miriam discovered that she had other news to share with her mother—she was pregnant again. As before, her parents were overjoyed. Miriam proudly presented her mother with the first picture of her grandchild, which was a sonogram of her yet-to-be born baby.

No matter what Miriam has gone through in her life, she knows Alma will be there for her. "My mother is my best friend. She's the person who has always been there for me, who supports me and listens to me when I cry. She doesn't always know the right thing to say, but she always says the right thing. I just hope that if I have a daughter, we can have the relationship my mom and I have." ■

The Greatest Love

Isabel Rivera

AND HER MOTHER,

Consuelo Alicia Rivera

Cocreator of the syndicated television series *Latin Access*, Isabel Rivera has always been a woman with a goal and a map to get there. She began her media career working at *PrimeTime Live*, *Good Morning America*, and *Live with Regis and Kathie Lee*. In addition to producing Emmy Award–winning programs, Isabel has been involved in producing programming about and for Latin audiences. ■ Of all the stories Isabel has covered as a news producer, the story that means the most to her is her mother's story of how she met and married her father.

THE GREATEST LOVE

Isabel's father, Elpidio Rivera, was returning home from his job as an Upper East Side doorman one hot summer night in August. As he crossed the street directly in front of his apartment building in Spanish Harlem, he was hit by a speeding police car. His body crashed into the windshield of the cruiser before being thrown to the other side of the street. The police car never stopped.

Isabel's mother heard the bang through the window of their seventeenth-floor apartment. She ran to the window and saw a body lying in the middle of the street. She didn't want to believe it was her husband. "I think she knew it was him, but just didn't want to accept it," Isabel recounts about the night she received the frantic call from her mother. "I came rushing over from across town but by the time I arrived my father had been taken away."

Isabel took her mother to the hospital, where they were told Elpidio had to have emergency surgery. His leg was crushed, as was his entire left side. He had lost a lot of blood. Isabel was the first to go in to see her father. Lying flat on a gurney, he was still bleeding from the head wounds. The first person he asked about was his wife. "You tell your mother I'm gonna be okay," he told Isabel as he took her hand into his own. "I don't want her to be scared. Don't leave her alone in the hospital because it's full of drug addicts. Go get her, and don't leave her alone for a minute," he implored.

Honoring her father's request, Isabel went to look for her mother. She found her in the ladies' bathroom, putting on lipstick.

"What are you doing?" Isabel asked her mother.

"I'm putting on lipstick," her mother answered, trying to be calm. "If your father sees me without lipstick, he'll be scared because he'll think something's wrong. I don't want him to worry that I'll be scared. I want him to feel as good as he can going into this and think that everything's going to be okay." Consuelo didn't want him to see her disheveled, something that did not surprise Isabel. Her parents have always been overprotective of each other.

"My father fell in love with my mother when he saw her photo on a relative's wall. As soon as he saw my mother's photo on her aunt's wall he wanted to meet her. Everybody kept saying they'd introduce them, but they never got around to it. Then one Christmas Eve he put on his purple shirt and his green suit, went to her house, and knocked on the door. He walked in, introduced himself to my grandfather.

" 'I want to meet your daughter,' he said. A year later they were married. And they have been married for thirty-nine years.

"I don't think my mother really had another serious boyfriend other than my father. My father said that when he met her he knew that she was a good woman and there was no need to look further. He thought she was beautiful and that she just had everything he was looking for. She always looked very nice; she was courteous and had good manners. She was like a dream come true for him.

"My parents rarely fought. They backed and supported each other. Even though they may not have agreed on everything the other spouse wanted to do, they always presented a united front to my sister and me. They always maintained a harmonious atmosphere.

"I think in a lot of ways I hope to have that same kind of relationship in my marriage. My mother and father have been together for so long, yet their relationship always seems so

Consuelo Alicia Rivera and her daughter, Isabel Rivera, sit on a park bench in New York City's Central Park.

as conscious as my mother is about getting my hair fixed. I think I'm more natural, but I do know that if my husband and I are going to a function, I want him to be happy and proud to introduce me."

Born in Puerto Rico, Consuelo came to New York City with her parents and only brother in the 1950s. The family settled in the Johnson Projects on 113th Street in East Harlem. Although she was barely six years old, Consuelo still recalls the discrepancies between the way she and her brother were treated. "Since my grandmother worked, my mother was a latchkey child" says Isabel, "which meant she had to come straight home from school, cook, and stay in the apartment until her parents came home from work. Because she was a girl she wasn't allowed to do the things that her brother was allowed to do, like play sports, go ice-skating, or go to the park."

Although Consuelo was a traditional woman who led a sheltered life, she knew early on that she wanted to raise her daughters differently. She wanted them to have the freedom she did not have while she was growing up. "My mother was a little bogged down in her childhood because my grandmother was very old-fashioned. 'You're a girl, you can't do this and you can't do that.' My mother wanted to give my sister and me an upbringing that was

new. Once a week they still have 'date night.' They go to the movies or have dinner. Some mornings they might take a walk and later during the day just have coffee together. I think that I was looking to find that in somebody, a partner who would want to do all that with me. I believe I found that in David."

Isabel is married to New York City news anchor David Ushery. Although their marriage is still young, she feels she has a strong role model in her mother's marriage to her father. "My mother always wanted to look good for my dad. I think in some way she's instilled that in me. I'm not always as very different than hers. That is why my mother always told us you could do anything that you want.

"My mother was always there for us when my sister and I came home from school. She always made time to read to us and participate in all of our activities. So I think if we have children some things would be really the same. Unlike my mother, I think I may have to work and my kids won't have the benefit of having an at-home mother. I definitely will not be the good cook that my mother is. And I don't know if I'd have the same patience my mother had for a lot of things.

"One of the lessons my mother taught me was that when you date somebody, see how they treat their mother, because ultimately, after the romance is over, you become the woman in their life. And if they treat their mother with respect and hold her in some type of regard, they'll treat you that way. And I think that that was an important lesson. I did look and I found that that was very true. I never met David's mother, but I know from the way he talks about her that he idolized her. And ultimately I wanted to have him talk about me that way.

"When my father was in the accident, the doctors didn't want my mother to sleep in the same bed during his recovery. So I had to go buy a mattress so that she could sleep on the floor next to him. And they'd fall asleep, kind of holding hands like he wanted her in his space and she wanted to be there. That's what love looks like. That's what I want in my life." ∎

Consuelo Alicia Rivera walks down a New York City street with her daughter, Isabel Rivera.

Ollita

Celia Cruz

AND HER MOTHER,

Catalina Alfonso

Known as the "Queen of Salsa," Celia Cruz is the most influential female in the history of Afro-Cuban music. A remarkable performer known for her amazing voice, Celia has recorded more than fifty albums and toured the world, performing with fellow legends Tito Puente, Willie Colon, Ray Barretto, and the Fania All-Stars. Among her many accolades, Celia won a Grammy, was honored with a star on the Hollywood Walk of Fame, was awarded an honorary doctorate of music by Yale University, and was given 1995's Billboard Lifetime Achievement Award. ■ Her mother, Catalina Alfonso, guided her daughter into the world of music, and her spirit continues to guide her even now.

OLLITA

ONE EVENING IN 1962, Celia Cruz was preparing herself for a performance. She had gone to a manicurist's shop downstairs from her apartment to get her nails done and she returned home a little earlier than expected. Trying to focus on the show that evening, Celia froze when she overheard her husband, Pedro Knight, talking to someone on the telephone: "No, look, Rosa, Celia's mother died last night," he said. "But I'm not going to tell Celia yet because she has a performance tonight." All she could do was cry.

Rather than cancel the show, Celia walked onto the stage that night and began to sing. To the audience's amazement, she burst into tears. "I was in my own world crying and crying," Celia explains. "I came out to sing and I began to cry. I would go backstage and cry, then come back out and sing again. My poor mother!" Pedro hadn't told the club's management or the press about Celia's loss, so it wasn't until days later that her fans found the source of her tears. Celia, however, would be haunted by her loss for the rest of her life.

"I left Cuba and my mother in 1960," Celia recalls. "When I left, she already had cancer. I left so that I could work and make money and send it to Cuba so that they could give my mother anything she wanted. Because pork has always been the cheapest meat, I wanted her to have the best—lobster, fish, and shrimp, anything! I would call back home and she would tell me not to worry, that she was taken care of. Other times I would call and she would be so weak that she could hardly talk. Once I asked to speak to the doctor and he said, 'She has cancer. She has two years to live, but if you take care

of her, she could last four.' She lasted four and a half. *La pobre!*"

Although Celia will not divulge the exact year of her birth, she was the second of four children born to Catalina Alfonso and Simon Cruz in the Santo Suárez neighborhood in Havana, Cuba. Celia's mother, Catalina, was born on April 30, 1900. Celia affectionately called her Ollita. "The whole world called her Ollita," she explains. "I never called her Mama. I think she got that name from a little boy that she raised. He was a white boy who didn't have a mother and she took him in. Maybe Catalina was too long for him to pronounce, so he called her Ollita. And now, the whole world calls her, 'Ollita, Ollita, Ollita . . .' "

Celia's amazing singing ability was evident ever since she was a child. Catalina encouraged her daughter to sing whenever they had visitors, and little Celia was happy to oblige. "My mother told everyone how much I liked to sing when I was a little girl," recalls Celia. "One time a friend of the family came by to visit and my mother said, 'Cantale, Celia' [sing for him, Celia] and I did. When I finished, the man was so delighted that he returned to our home and gave me a pair of shoes as a gift." Celia sang from the time that she was an infant. "My grandmother told my mother that I was going to work at night because when I was nine or ten months old I used to wake up in the middle of the night singing."

When she was six years old, Celia went to live with her aunt, Ana. "Ana was the one who raised me until she moved back to Pinar de Rio and I went back to live with my mother," she explains. The special bond between Celia and her aunt began when her aunt's own daughter died. "My aunt was like a mother to me," Celia says. "Before I was born, Ana had a daughter who fell ill. The doctors told her that her daughter was going to die. They told her that her daughter was returning to dust. So when the little girl died, Ana went up to the coffin, spread her fingers, and broke them. She believed that in doing this she would recognize her daughter when she was reincarnated. During that time my mother was pregnant with me and when I was born, I was born with my fingers very crooked. You can see it when my fingers are spread. I am the reincarnation of her daughter. That's why my aunt Ana loved me so much."

The supernatural bond between Celia, her mother, and her aunt is one that all three women acknowledged. "When my mother would see my aunt coming from the river, she would tell me, 'Listen, your mother is coming.' And she has remained like a mother to me all my life."

Once Celia went to live with her aunt Ana, she took the young teenager to ballrooms, cabarets, and radio and television stations to compete and sing with various popular orchestras. Her second mother, Ana, was very supportive of her singing and would

Celia Cruz looks at a portrait of her mother, Catalina Alfonso.

take any opportunity to make sure that Celia showed her talent. "One day, Titi Ana took me to a television station, an *emisora*, called La Casa de la Biblia," Celia recalls. "I started to sing a song, but I didn't move. My aunt told me, '*Ay*, my niece! You have to dance. You have to do something! You can't sing that *guaracha* and not move at all.' I was shy. I really did like to dance, but not in front of people. She said, 'You have to dance because if you don't move you're not expressing anything to the public.' So from that moment on, I began to dance when I sang."

Soon, Celia was getting help and advice on her singing career from everyone in her family—everyone except her father. "He didn't want me to be a singer. I don't blame him because there was a time in the world when women who wanted to become artists had to have sex with the owner of a club or station. And that's what he thought women had to do to get ahead in show business. So my mother, that saint, told me, 'Sweetheart, you go ahead and forget it. I'll deal with him.'

"My father was a *fogonero* and he worked on the railroad. When notices of my performances started coming out in the newspaper, people would tell my father, 'Look, Simon. There's this girl in the newspaper that has the same last name as you.' And he would say, 'Yes, but she is not related to me.' Well, one day he sat down to talk to me and he told me, 'Look, I didn't want you to be an artist because of this and this.' The next day, a friend of his came and said, 'Look, Simon, look at the picture of that girl I told you about.' In the newspaper was a photograph of Celia along with a glowing review of her singing. Her father read over the article and told his friend, 'Yes, she's my daughter. So what?' " Celia says, "It gave him joy because it said I was a good singer. After that he was convinced that I could do it."

In retrospect, Celia believes that her father wanted to embrace his daughter's singing because he knew that he was ill. Before she left Cuba, the doctor had warned Celia about her father's impending death, so she had left money for his funeral and burial. "Back then people would die young, and my father was already old. He was seventy-eight when he died. My family didn't tell me anything because I was scheduled to debut on a show and they said, 'Why should we tell her if they aren't going to revive him?' They told me a month later, 'Look, your father died.' I am grateful that they didn't tell me because I would have been in bad shape when I had to perform, like I was when my mother died."

Despite the fact that Celia does not consider herself a political woman, politics have had an enormous impact on her life. Because of Celia's defection from Cuba, Castro refused to allow the singer to return home to visit her mother in the hospital or to attend her funeral. While Cuba will always remain an enormous part of who she is, Celia has decided that when she dies she wants to be buried in her adopted home, America. In many ways, it seemed tragedy was waiting for Celia to leave Cuba before it struck. Just as she left for her singing debut in Mexico, the doctors admitted her mother to the hospital. Catalina wasn't happy because she felt that she wouldn't see her daughter again.

"I used to call the hospital and she would say, 'Oh, my daughter! How are you? I want to see you, but I know that's not possible.' Other mothers would have said, 'You have to come.' But she was a saint. Then she started talking nonsense. I say nonsense because she would be talking to me and then she would say, 'No, because Saint Lazarus . . .' I don't know what she was talking about. So my family would take the phone from her. I asked them to send me a picture of her but they didn't send it because she ended up not looking anything like herself. When a person has cancer, they get all disfigured. So, I prefer to remember her like she used to be."

Celia remembers her mother as a woman full of life and song. "My mother loved to sing and she had a beautiful voice." The love of music she learned from her mother would ultimately prove more valuable than the things she didn't learn. "My mother didn't teach me to cook. They would cook everything for me. I don't know what my poor mother thought about me. Maybe she visualized that I would not have to cook. When we got married I said, 'Look, Pedro, that kitchen is going to die of laughter.' And Pedro said, 'No, it's not going to die of laughter. You are going to learn.' I cook for my husband because he taught me how to cook."

As a youth, Celia continued with her studying as well as her singing. She sang for money in amateur shows to buy her schoolbooks for the República de Mexico public school in Havana. "When I graduated, a teacher asked me to sing at a party that day. And I sang there. Afterwards, we sat side by side and I told her, 'Doctor, I have to look for a job now.' And she told me, 'Look, girl, keep singing and forget about teaching. One day you're going to make in one night what I make in one month.' "

Celia took her teacher's advice and began looking at her singing as a serious career. Against her father's wishes, she dropped out of the Escuela Normal para Maestros where she was studying to be a teacher of literature and enrolled at the Conservatory of Music to study voice and music theory. Following her heart, Celia became far more than what she wanted—she is a singer, but she is also a legend, known throughout the world for her contribution to Latin music.

Despite her mastery of music, she found there were things she could not achieve. "I love children and I've wanted children all my life," says Celia. "But God did not give them to me. When I saw that I could not have kids, that they were not coming, I went to a couple of doctors to see what was wrong. They checked me to see if they could find the problem. Both times I came out dead from the procedures. After the second checkup, I came home so sick my husband told me, 'Chica, don't worry. I love you just the way you are.' He has children from his first marriage. He said, 'I love you like this. You don't have to go anymore if you don't want to.'

"I thought, well, they're not coming. Then I realized that God knows what He's doing. Even though somebody told me, 'No, God doesn't get involved in that.' I know that God is involved in everything. He's right here right now. So, I think, it's good that He didn't give me a child. I have nephews and nieces and I love them a lot. They are really nice. They don't forget my birthday or Pedro's. They are good and grateful.

"My mother was the one who brought me into this world. She's responsible for me being here. The days when she was in critical condition, when she became sicker, I had a dream about her. I saw her passing by the sidewalk in front of where I was. I didn't see her face. And I said, 'Ollita, don't leave me.' And she said, 'No, baby, I am always going to be with you.' She hadn't died yet when I had that dream. But I knew that if you dream of someone and you don't see their face, it's a bad sign."

Celia believes that her mother watches over her and is by her side every time she opens her mouth to sing. "When I'm about to sing, I call her, 'Ollita, I want you to help me.' I still call her so she can be there with me and so that I won't lose my nerve. I want my mother's spirit to stay with me. Ollita, my mother, please stay with me until the day I die because I'm coming to you."

Despite the years, the distance, and the politics that have separated mother and daughter, Celia will always have Ollita. "My mother was a saint. She should have a crown up there. The story of my mother and me is a beautiful one." ■

Celia Cruz holds a portrait of her mother, Catalina Alfonso.

Home Sweet Home

Rossana Rosado

AND HER MOTHER,

Luz Rosado

Rossana is the first woman publisher and chief executive officer of *El Diario/La Prensa*, the oldest Spanish-language newspaper in the country and the largest Spanish-language daily newspaper in the northeast. Rossana has long been involved in making a positive impact on the lives of others, having served as a reporter, an Emmy Award–winning producer, and as vice president for public affairs of the Health and Hospitals Corporation for the City of New York. ■ Like her daughter, Luz used words to positively influence her daughter's life in ways she was unable to impact her own.

HOME SWEET HOME

Luz Rosado was not happy to see her daughter pack her bags to move out of the family house. Even if the move meant her eldest daughter, Rossana, would only be four short blocks away. "My mother was so upset," Rossana recalls. "It wasn't so much about her wanting me to stay home until I got married, it was because she thought there was so much danger out there. But I was already a professional. So I found an apartment four blocks away and I moved out right before my twenty-fifth birthday. It was really tough for her. I don't remember her ever visiting me in that apartment."

Having her first child leave the nest was especially difficult for Luz because of how hard she and her husband had to work for their home and what that home meant to her. A house was a symbol of security for Luz. And security was something she wanted to provide for her daughters.

Born in Coamo, Puerto Rico, Luz and her family came to the States when she was twelve years old. When Luz was about to graduate high school in 1958, her family began hinting that she should consider marrying her boyfriend. "She really didn't want to get married right away. She wanted to wait because she had a job, but in the late 50's you didn't have long courtships." Luz began to really feel the pressure when her family threw a surprise engagement party for her and her boyfriend before they were actually engaged. And marriage also meant a place of her own, so she gave in and agreed to set a date.

The couple was married in 1960. While her husband served in the army, Luz found herself looking forward to being a wife and running her own household. But she was always independent and fully planned on a career as a working girl. Her plans took a drastic turn, however, with the birth of Rossana a short year into her marriage.

"My mother stayed home after she had me, which was what was expected of her, but she always wanted to go back to work. Every time she was ready to go back to work, she got pregnant again. She always refers to those years as 'very unhappy years.' She told us that she loved us, but those were difficult years for her because she wound up having four children, which is a big family in any generation."

Not only did Luz have to put her education and career plans on hold; she also had to wait for a home to call her own.

"We lived in one of three apartments in my grandfather's house. For most of my childhood, my father worked for my mother's father. My grandfather had a bodega and at one point he had two bodegas. In our

MAMÁ · *Latina Daughters Celebrate Their Mothers*

community, that was like being rich. But we were never rich because of the way bodegas were run, they barely provided a livelihood for my father and two uncles. My father worked for him, but because my father wasn't his son, he didn't profit from the business. It was my mother who was concerned that my father didn't make a lot of money. She told him, 'You have to get out of there because we're never going to get ahead.' "

Luz always planned ahead to secure her family's future. At her urging, Rossana's father stopped working for his father-in-law and got a job driving a truck, a union job with health benefits. "My father drove a truck for twenty-something years until he retired two years ago. Within two years of my father starting his new job and my mother going back to work, they were able to buy their own house in the Bronx."

For Luz, owning a house meant everything. Being a home owner gave her a strong sense of worth. It also meant the first step in achieving the American dream. "We moved into the house in 1971. That was such a big deal for them. They were pretty young with four children, but they got their own house. It was tough at first because they had no credit and they qualified for nothing close to a mortgage. I think the house cost about twenty-four thousand dollars."

If not for the eight years Luz took off to raise her children, she would have had a very different life. "If she hadn't had all of us kids, I think she probably would've been a professional in some kind of office environment," explains Rossana. "She typed very fast and, right out of high school, she went to work at New York Hospital. When she went back to work eight years later, she went to work at another hospital. She worked at Mount Sinai as a registrar for about seventeen years.

"The eight years that my mother was out of work raising us was a very sad part of her history," says Rossana. "She very much believed in women preparing for careers. She always counseled my sister and I that no matter what you do, you go to college."

Rossana was the first person in her extended family to do so. "When I decided to go to college it was very scary for my parents because they didn't know if they could afford it. And of course they couldn't, but they did it anyway. It's interesting that my sister and I were both encouraged to pursue higher education because even though my mother would've preferred that my brothers went to college, she didn't push them as much and they didn't go."

Rossana ended up going to Pace University in White Plains, New York. "I was about half an hour away from our house in the Bronx. That's how far they would let me go. When my sister went to college, I had already broken them in, so she got to go to college in Rhode Island. I had never been apart from my parents before. We didn't do summer camp or stuff like that, so the distance was a big concern to them."

Despite her wanting to have her daughter nearby, Luz always gave Rossana her unwavering support throughout her college years.

"My mother never encouraged us to ever get married," says Rossana. "In fact, she was always discouraging us about getting married and letting somebody take care of you. She didn't do this from a point of bitterness, because my parents had a good marriage—going on forty-one years— even though we wanted to be the Brady Bunch, we had a very happy childhood.

We didn't grow up seeing marriage as a bad thing, but my mother was always clear that she felt she married too young and didn't want us to make the same mistake."

Sometimes, when growing up as a second-generation Latina you hear conflicting messages from your mother. Latinas are taught by their mothers to be independent career women who shouldn't rely on a man for survival. But at the same time, they are considered a failure if they get to a certain age and are not married with children. Although Luz was determined to encourage her daughters to finish college and have their own careers before getting married, Rossana received conflicting advice from her grandmother. "My grandmother was always asking me, 'Now that you have college and now that you have done all this stuff, when are you going to settle down and have kids?' I always regret that I got married seven months after my grandmother died.

"What's funny is that at the same time, I remember my grandmother saying to me, 'No matter what, you should always have your own bank account.' She had her own bank account. My grandfather was a businessman and when he died he left some property, but he didn't leave a lot of money. But when my grandmother died she left a bank book and a list of how her money should be divided up. It was always clear that as a woman you had to be self-sufficient no matter

what, whether the marriage was good or bad."

Navigating the unfamiliar course of college was one thing, but making her mother understand what she was doing with that college education was even tougher for Rossana. "I think it was tough for my mother because I chose this career that was so different," she explains. "She didn't really know anything about the media and neither did I. When I worked at CBS, I went through the training for desk assistant. My mother bought me some business suits and helped me get ready for the job. Then two weeks after the training was over they put me into my regular slot, which was midnight to seven A.M. My mother could not understand why I was required to work those horrible hours. She would say, 'We sent you to college and you have to work the night shift?' My father wanted to drive me to work every night because they thought it was not safe for a woman to take the subway at that time of the night. But he wasn't always able to drive me to work because he had to get up real early to go to work himself. So I had no choice but to get on the subway. Even though I was out of college and already working, my mother was always very worried. I was very sheltered in a positive way."

Years after she started working, Rossana realized that she was making more money than both her parents had made while they were raising their four kids. "I was making more money than they did and I thought I had no money. My mother encouraged me. She was happy that I had a career because it was a step further than she went—a big step further than she went."

For Rossana, there were definite rules she had to follow growing up that didn't change very much even when she was out of college and in the workforce. "I was working at *El Diario* as a reporter and if I had a date, no matter how late that date went, I always came home. I never spent the night out. It would never enter my mind to try to spend the night out or to walk out of the house without telling anybody where I was going. If my parents were having company I couldn't just leave the house and say, 'Okay, bye. I have my own plans.' "

After a while, Rossana started to feel the pressure of living under her mother's roof. "I really felt that I needed to be out of that house. There was no space for me. It wasn't like I had my own room; I shared a room with my sister. Because all of us drove, there were six cars in that one driveway. Something had to give. I was going to be twenty-five and everybody I worked with was so much older. Many had left Puerto Rico or Latin America and were on their own in New York. I admired their independence, so I started looking for an apartment to move out."

As it turned out, however, Rossana would only stay in her apartment a short five months because of a surprise her parents had for her. They had decided to move into their weekend house in upstate New York. "I moved back home and I shared the house with my sister and one of my brothers. My parents said, 'This is the mortgage. You guys take care of it.'

"Years later when my sister and I discussed it, we decided it was the safe thing for them to do. When they gave us the house, that meant they knew where we were and they knew we had a roof over our heads. I always laugh when I tell people that instead of us leaving home, my parents left home. But I think they also did it strategically to keep us all together and to make us responsible, because since we have to pay a mortgage, we just couldn't be out there acting crazy."

Rossana reports, "The house is still in my family. I lived there for many years with my sister and when I got married, my husband moved in and my sister moved out. Then when I moved out, my sister moved back in. Since then, she bought it from my parents and she's still living there. My mother told me once in recent years that it never felt like Christmas to her unless she was in the house on Taylor Avenue, her first home."

In a sense, Luz made sure that the home she created for her family would continue on without her. In a reversal of events, Rossana is now the one having a hard time seeing someone leave the nest. Rossana burst into tears when her mother informed her earlier this year that she and Rossana's father had purchased some land in Florida and that they would be building a house. "All I could do was cry and cry. I can't believe she is leaving us," Rossana says.

But a lesson that both women have learned from each other is that a home can only be truly found by leaving the nest. ■

Keep the Faith

Columba Bush

AND HER MOTHER,

Josefina Gallo

Born in Leon, Guanajato, Mexico, Columba Garnica Gallo married John Ellis ("Jeb") Bush in 1974 and became the First Lady of Florida when Jeb was elected governor of Florida in 1998. Columba has been active as a spokesperson for Informed Families of Florida, a nonprofit organization involved in educating families about drug abuse. She is also the cofounder of the Children's Cultural Education Fund of the Ballet Folklorico, the national dance troupe of Mexico. ■ While Columba's responsibilities have put unwanted miles between mother and daughter, Josefina Gallo's life of faith continues to inspire and drive her daughter forward.

KEEP THE FAITH

BORN IN 1922 in Leon, Mexico, Columba's mother, Josefina Gallo, was raised as a very religious girl in a very religious town. In those days, the town of Leon held mass every day and everyone was expected to attend. And as expected, Josefina was enrolled in Catholic school and grew up under its protective wings. She lived with her godfather, who was overprotective of her and very strict.

Columba describes her mother's life as that of a sheltered young woman who didn't have much opportunity to meet potential suitors. "My mother wasn't very social, which is probably why she got married when she was twenty-nine. My mother's godfather was selling lamp oil to a man from a nearby town. This man had a son about the same age as my mother, so they thought it was a good idea to arrange for them to marry. I don't think she was ever really in love with him, but she's been always there for him, accepting and giving. She said, 'Well, I'll try my best.' "

Struggling to live up to the expectations of her family, church, and community, Josefina eventually realized that she had done everything she could to make the best of an unworkable situation. So, with all of the pressure and three young children, Josefina decided to divorce her husband in 1963. "When my parents divorced, it was a really big deal for their families and friends. To get divorced in the sixties in Mexico was a sin. But my mother always survives. I don't know how she does it, but she's a survivor. What I think is fabulous is that the divorce didn't bother her at all. After the divorce, she would continue doing exactly the same things

she did before. She would go to mass and continue to go to every religious celebration. She didn't say, 'Well, this is a bad situation and I should try to get away from here.' "

Not letting a bad situation stop her or define her is one of the great gifts Josefina passed on to her daughter. Seeing her mother step over obstacles gave Columba her sense of independence. "I'm a very independent person because of my mother. She always encouraged us to be very independent—she probably didn't have any other alternative." Despite the pressure to conform, Josefina has never seen religion or her faith as restrictive. On the contrary, her faith has always been liberating. "My mother raised me as a very religious person but without all the overwhelming things, like dictating how we should dress. She always was very open-minded."

Growing up in a small Mexican town didn't leave Columba and her siblings with many diversions. But like her mother, Columba says that suited her fine. "There was not much to do, but I have never been a social person. I had four or five friends at the most. I would invite them home to drink Coca-Cola and listen to music. My mother was a bit more social than I am. I think it's just my personality. I just love silence. I like to read a good book and go for a walk.

"There was a very big difference between how my brother was treated and how my sister and I were treated. It's part of our culture that the mothers think boys are so special and wonderful and they treat them in a very special way. But despite that, my mother taught all of us that education is the most important thing because you will then always have something to rely on, something that no one can take away from you. And she expected the same from all three of us. She told my sister and I, 'You have to have your education because you are always going to need that. Even if you marry a prince, you still need to know your skills.'"

Columba met her prince in 1971 when Jeb Bush came to Leon, Mexico, to teach English in an exchange program. Three years later, the couple married in Austin, Texas, and eventually relocated to Miami, Florida, where they raised their three children. Following an unsuccessful bid in 1994 for governor, Columba's husband was elected to be the forty-third governor of the state of Florida in 1998. It was a move that forever changed Columba's life.

"No one prepares you for a life in politics. But what was helpful to me was having a very strong faith that I got from my mother. I came into politics without being prepared, but when you have a very strong faith, you just don't lose hope. You may think, 'Things are really bad now, but I'm going to pray.' And you really pray, 'God, please help me with this situation.' Then you get clarity and understanding. One of my prayers is, 'If I'm here, it has to be for a reason. So please help me.' There are a lot of moments that you just need prayer. My mother gave me a good example through her faith. I'm sure my mother spent hours praying and she never loses hope, which is very amazing.

A photograph of Josefina Gallo held by her daughter, Columba Bush.

"I try to tell my mother about all the things that I learned from her and the things that I admire about her, but she doesn't get it because she doesn't even imagine what life in politics is like. Being in politics is like having a child. You can't know what it's like until you have one. You can't describe a political life. You can't say, 'It's like this,' or 'It's like that.' You have to be part of it. The minute that my husband was elected, everything changed in my life."

Unfortunately, one of the big changes that Columba has

Columba Bush at home in Florida.

to contend with is that she and her mother don't get to spend much time together. Her mother's health has been deteriorating rapidly because of diabetes. "Since my husband ran for office for the first time, we live under so much pressure that I don't see my mother as often as I'd like. Most people don't understand and don't believe it. They'll say, 'Can you come for dinner?' and I'll say, 'I don't think so because we have a crisis here.' And we have crisis after crisis after crisis after crisis. And these are things I can't say to my mother because of her health. She would only worry more and more.

"My mother had been living in Mexico and she became very sick. She came to live in Miami with my sister when I was living in Venezuela. That is when we discovered that she had diabetes. The next thing I know, she was getting worse and worse, about five years ago, she lost her leg. So she's been through so much with her health that of course I don't want to give her any more problems."

Thinking of the many spiritual and cultural things she received from her mother, Columba talks about what her children have and have not received from her. "George, my oldest son, is good about speaking Spanish, but Noelle and Jebby still have a long way to go because they understand it, but they don't speak it. It's a different time today. My daughter and I were very close until she turned sixteen. With my mother and myself, there's no generation gap. I mean, we like the same movies and we like the same music. Believe it or not, I'm old-fashioned here. It's like good traditions. If they have a celebration at church, my mother and I would both go and enjoy it the same. If there are things that are important and big for my mother, I would enjoy them too. What I found out with my daughter is that the difference between generations today, unfortunately, is huge. All the patterns that separate parents and children start happening. We don't sit and watch movies together or listen to the same music. We spend less and less time with the children, so you start losing that communication with them. They talk about certain songs and you say, 'What are you talking about? I never heard that in my life.' So it's a shame. And it happens in Mexico, too. I have met a lot of American women, from all nationalities, and we all have this same thing in common everywhere. We probably have different ways of expressing it but many of the mothers I have met have gone through the same thing."

As Columba moves forward in her life, she realizes just how similar she is to her mother. And like her mother, she too has discovered that she has the faith to step over the obstacles and uncertainties she encounters in her life. "My mother went through a lot but I just have to thank her for all of the things that she went through. She was a survivor and is still surviving." ■

Quiet Strength

Yvette Martas

AND HER MOTHER,

Magdalena Martas

Yvette Martas is an instructor of obstetrics and gynecology at the New York University School of Medicine. In her position at the NYU Medical Center, Yvette handles every aspect of a woman's sexual and reproductive life from counseling preteen mothers to helping older couples have their first baby. One of the few Latina doctors at NYU, she takes particular interest in counseling young Latinas whose cultural backgrounds many times influence the decisions they make regarding their reproductive lives. ■ While Yvette has flown to a level of success beyond her mother's dreams, it is because of Magdalena Martas's support that her daughter has the freedom to soar.

QUIET STRENGTH

YVETTE MARTAS grew up feeling she was the son her father never had. Not only did she physically look like her father, she also had the same focused determination and stubborn personality. "I felt that I had nothing that my mother had. Nothing. I thought that my second sister, Magda, was the one that had everything my mother had—her creativity, her beauty, and her voice. Now I think I'm very much a combination of both of them." As an adult, Yvette realizes that her father was her professional and intellectual role model, while her mother has always been her spiritual guru and anchor.

Yvette's parents had a very traditional marriage. Magdalena was a housewife who dedicated her life to taking care of her husband and raising their three daughters. "I didn't know what my mother's strengths were when I was younger. She spoke some English, but it was very broken English. She had to navigate changing school systems, getting her daughters into a better school, talking to teachers, all with her broken English. I think she took on these challenges for the same reasons I do things—I don't want to have fear.

"My mother never learned to drive. I think she's afraid to drive because my father may have criticized her at some point. Even without driving, though, she did everything to get us to wherever we had to get to. Somewhere along the way, I learned how to get around the New York City train system from her. It had to be her because it wasn't my father. I remember she was the one who got on the train with me to go to Bronx Science, the high school I wanted to go to, and many other places around the city.

"But once we became independent enough that we could manage the system on our own, my mother abdicated all her functions. She stopped going out and getting around the city on her own. I don't understand that. She'll get out to go shopping in the neighborhood, but she won't negotiate the system. My mother says I'm very much like my father, and so with that excuse she felt that I was someone who could take care of herself. And I was a very stubborn kid in many ways. When I wanted something, I would get it for the most part.

While Yvette has always been independent, she has discovered that she has had to depend on her mother for support no one else could give. "My mother provides the care and the love that gets you through those times when you feel you can't do it anymore. One of her sayings to me is, 'Grano a grano llena la gallina el buche' [roughly translated as 'Little by little you get to where you want to go']. It's funny because I've never asked her where she's wanted to go. That is something that I regret a little bit. My mother has a beautiful voice and I know she wanted to be a singer. Knowing how intelligent my mother is, at some point in her life she must have questioned her role or desired something different. I realize now that she postponed her own dreams to allow her three daughters to pursue their dreams."

Yvette's father was a very different type of influence in her life. "I was very much afraid of my father. He was the law. When he came home, he was the kind of guy that if we were watching cartoons and he wanted to watch baseball, we turned the channel. We only had one TV in the house.

"By the time I was born, he was working in the baking industry. He started working for many companies baking bread for school systems. He got into the union as a delegate and, little by little, he became very popular. He's been the union president for years. He still goes out and unionizes and negotiates contracts. He's a very active person."

Yvette credits her father's success to her mother's ability to quietly encourage and push him. "She's good that way. She can really tell you, 'You can do it,' without actually telling you. If you tell her, 'I want to do this,' then she'll provide you with the avenue to do it. She's not going to tell you, 'You can.' So it's a quiet support, very quiet."

Yvette's education was always very important to her mother. Even with her limited knowledge of the process, Madgalena is responsible for making certain all three of her daughters had the opportunity to go college. Yvette ended up going to an all-girl high school, Academy of Mount St. Ursula, on a full scholarship. "I didn't want to go there because there were only a handful of Puerto Rican girls there and maybe three or four African-American girls, everybody else was white." Her mother helped her understand that was not a reason not to have a good education that would prepare her for college.

When it came time to apply to college, Yvette had to decipher the complicated college application on her own. Unable

to turn to her parents for advice on what schools she should apply to, Yvette set her mind on Yale. Her father did not understand why she wanted to go to college three hours away from home when there were perfectly good colleges right there in the Bronx. It was her mother who finally convinced her father to let her go.

Magdalena quietly supported her daughter by gently pushing her toward her life's work in medicine. Yvette says, "I always had some sort of civic consciousness when I was a kid. Even in grammar school I drew her this big poster of a guy who's on drugs and I taped it and put it in the hallway downstairs by the mailboxes of our building in the projects so people could see what drugs do to you.

"Medicine is a vocation for me. I don't think it was a choice that I made; it was a choice that was made for me. While in college I didn't take any science courses because I didn't have any intentions of going to medical school. After graduating with

Her mother suffered along with Yvette through the arduous nights of studying through medical school. "She was there moment by moment—if I had to get up early to go to the library, she would get up earlier, wake me up, and make sure I got out."

Even after Yvette began her own successful medical practice, she discovered that she still had to turn to her mother's quiet strength. It was this strength that helped Yvette get through the difficulty of trying to have a child of her own. After suffering a number of miscarriages and several years of fertility treatments, Magdalena provided spiritual comfort to Yvette and her husband throughout these difficult times.

"I used to find it so hard to believe that I may not be able to experience that part of being a woman. Sometimes I would ask myself, 'What did I do in a previous life? Did I do something that somehow has forced me to come to this?' That was a very negative way to think about it sometimes, but it was a hard reality to deal with.

"I remember working with a young family when the young mother had to be admitted because she had gone into

a degree in sociology I went back to school to take all my premed requirement courses, while working full-time for the City of New York. All of this was a little confusing for my mother. She was concerned about me going down a path that she was unfamiliar with. She would say, '¿*Pero mi'ja tanto tiempo en la universidad y ahora es que te decidiste hacer esto?*' [But *mi'ja*, such a long time in the university and now you decide to do this?]

"When I finished my courses and began the process of getting to medical school, my mother was very supportive. She cooked for me; she did what a mother always does. This was very important to me. I know that when I got home no matter what hour of the night it was, I always had a warm plate of food ready and my mother was sitting down by the kitchen table asking me how did my day go? She couldn't ask me about what I was learning, but she would always ask how my day went. That was all I needed to feel all right. When I had to go take those hard exams she would tell me the typical Puerto Rican '*Ay, ay, ay bendito*, why do you have to take so many exams again?' "

premature labor. We got her to thirty five and a half weeks and she started to contract. Her mother was with her all the time. Her husband was great. They came every day. And she had a sister who's fantastic. There was nothing this woman could want for. I bonded a great deal with them and they with me because we were Latin.

"Finally the night I was on call, it was okay for her to deliver. We took her to her room where she could just labor quietly, and all this woman was focused on and all her husband was focused on was, 'Baby, be okay, baby be okay.' They were cheering the baby on. The baby was born, and her mother fell to her knees thanking God and got up from her knees and kissed her daughter, saying, 'Thank you so much for this beautiful thing that you have given us, you've worked so hard.' Her husband was crying and the room was just so joyous. Although I was overjoyed for that family, I felt a little sadness afterwards because I felt that was as close as I was ever going to get to that experience.

"The issue of motherhood touches my heart because I don't want to have a child after my parents are gone. Having a baby is a family event and I think it's a joy that we should experience together.

"I have some guilt because my parents are not Abuelo and Abuelita. I think about that a lot. But it's not something my parents put on me. My mother has helped me realize that delivering babies is a gift in its own right. That perhaps helping other women give birth is my way of experiencing the miracle of birth." Yvette smiles and adds, "And I still get to maintain my figure.

"I have a supportive husband, great friends, and a strong and loving mother. I realized I can have a rich and fulfilling life with my family whether or not I have a biological child. My mother's spiritual insight has taught me that my family is complete." ■

Dr. Yvette Martas and her mother,
Magdalena Martas.

A Living Memorial

Belkys Diaz

AND HER MOTHER,

Carmen Diaz

Nancy Diaz had lived in the United States less than three years when she was killed along with nearly 3,000 others in the terrorist attacks on the World Trade Center on September 11, 2001. ■ Surviving her heroically is her sister, Belkys Diaz, who, along with her mother, Carmen Diaz, have taken on the responsibility of raising Nancy's five-year-old daughter, Amanda. Together, these women continue a tradition of nourishing and nurturing their families, regardless of the hardships or tragedies that befall them.

A LIVING MEMORIAL

AT 7:00 A.M. ON TUESDAY, September 11, 2001, Nancy Diaz arrived for her job at the Windows on the World restaurant in the World Trade Center's north tower. Typically, Nancy didn't show up for her job as a kitchen assistant until 10:30 A.M., but she came in early because she wanted to have that afternoon free to prepare for her trip to the Dominican Republic. Her daughter, Amanda, was eagerly awaiting her mother's arrival that Friday for her birthday in Santo Domingo.

That morning, Nancy would have been able to see a spectacular view from the restaurant's 106th floor window on what was a picture-perfect New York City day. At 8:45 A.M., she was tending the restaurant's breakfast buffet when American Airlines Flight 11, carrying ninety-two people from Boston to Los Angeles, crashed into the tower. Suddenly, everything changed forever.

Along with thousands of others, Nancy's mother, Carmen, and her sister, Belkys Diaz, found their world violently turned upside down. Belkys was not only Nancy's little sister, she was her roommate and best friend.

Belkys and Nancy were born and raised in the Dominican Republic and shared everything. Belkys remembers her childhood as being carefree, and she remembers being very devoted to both her sister and her mother. "We were both very attached to my mother. When she came to the United States, we had never been separated for such a long time."

The two sisters were left behind in Santo Domingo when their mother followed their father in emigrating to the United States. Like many immigrants who want to bring their families to the States, the Diaz family had to contend with the complicated rules of the Immigration and Naturalization Service (INS). Because the INS requires immigrants to have a sponsor who can demonstrate the ability to support them, families wishing to immigrate are often forced to break up in order to come to the States. One member immigrates, who then sponsors another member, who then is able to sponsor another.

After Belkys's father arrived in New York City, he sponsored his wife, his son, and then Nancy. Belkys recalls, "My sister came here before I did, because my father sponsored her. Then I joined the rest of the family."

Having her family reunited, Carmen began working in a factory where she made Everlast boxing gloves. Seeing how difficult life was for her family in America, Belkys admits that she was disillusioned. "It is different here in the U.S. People think that you come to America to

seek better opportunities, but that is a misconception. In Santo Domingo, I was free and independent. I did not lack for anything. I had a very successful business selling shoes and bags door to door." For Belkys, opportunity has not been easy to find in her new home.

Nancy, however, was excited about the opportunities that stretched out before her. By the time her sister arrived in New York, Nancy had obtained a job at the prestigious Windows on the World and had already applied to bring her three-year-old daughter, Amanda, to the States. When the

Belkys Diaz with her mother, Carmen Diaz, and her niece, Amanda. A portrait of her sister, Nancy Diaz, hangs over Belkys's shoulder in the photograph on the previous page.

sisters learned that the request had been denied, Nancy was undeterred. She submitted another application and began planning what was to be only her second trip to visit her daughter back in Santo Domingo. The occasion was Amanda's fifth birthday and her mother had planned to give her daughter an unforgettable party.

On that fateful Tuesday morning, Nancy was one of thirty-eight Windows on the World employees who lost their lives. After the attacks on the Twin Towers, Amanda was granted a humanitarian visa and her grandfather flew to the Dominican Republic to bring her to the place her mother dreamed of bringing her—her new home in the United States.

Because of the unique set of circumstances surrounding her immigration, when asked, Amanda will say she has many *"mamis."* In many ways, Amanda's life demonstrates the power and resilience of Latina motherhood. In addition to her real mother, Amanda has surrogate mothers in her aunt Belkys, the aunt who raised her in the Dominican Republic ("Mami Maritza"), and her grandmother Carmen.

Carmen has happily taken on the responsibility of raising her granddaughter. Belkys says, "My mother takes her to school each morning, just like she did for Nancy and I. It is not a problem for her. She has been able to ease right into the role of being a mother; she's like any of the other mothers at the school. If Amanda has to go to the doctor, my mother is the one who takes her. This is something very normal for her."

If the Diaz women have been able to create a sense of normalcy for Amanda, Belkys hopes to also create a sense of normalcy for herself. Like her sister before her, Belkys came to America with the hopes of being able to sponsor her son, now being raised by an aunt in Santo Domingo. Recently, Belkys was informed that her son's visa had not been approved. "In a way I don't know what it is like to be a mother because my son has been raised by my aunt since he was two months old," Belkys says. But just as her older sister persevered, Belkys plans to reapply and looks forward to being with her child again. "I imagine that it will be something very special."

Amanda has few questions about what happened to her mother on September 11. "She knows what happened, but she does not ask" says Belkys. "If she did, I would have no words to respond to her. The truth is that she is five years old. She goes to school and plays. She sees a psychologist and, as she grows up, she will forget. She was three years old when she was separated from her mother, so her memory of Nancy is through pictures and calls and letters. If she was eight or ten years old, she would have many more questions to ask."

While adjusting to life without Nancy, her mother, sister, and daughter find that moving forward is a challenge, but it is a challenge they face with hope and confidence. They know that even if one of them falls, the others will be there to take her place. ■

Home Is Where the Heart Is

Jaci Velásquez

AND HER MOTHER,

Diana Catherine Velásquez

The youngest of six children, Jaci Velásquez is the daughter of traveling Christian evangelists and musicians. In 1996, Jaci's first album, *Heavenly Place*, was released and caught the Christian music world by storm. Certified gold, the album spawned a book and three number-one singles. Since then, Jaci has released four albums, including the platinum *Llegar a Ti*, and has performed at the 2001 presidential inaugural ceremony. ■ Jaci's mother, Diana Catherine Velásquez, has shephered her daughter's career every step of the way, from its humble beginning to its current heavenly place.

I N M A N Y W A Y S , Diana Catherine Velásquez has groomed her daughter for her music career all her life. From the time she was three years old, Diana knew her daughter had an innate, God-given ability to sing. And more than merely being a singer, Diana knew her baby girl was going to be a star. "My mother always thought that I was going to be famous," says Jaci. "Ever since I was a little girl she always said, 'I know my daughter is going to do something where she has to sign autographs.' She would tell me that and I would say, 'Nooo!' But ever since I was three or four years old, she would make me sign my name J-A-C-I, because she said Jacquelyn is too long. 'You're gonna have long autograph lines so you have to have a short name.' So since then, I never signed my name 'Jacquelyn Velásquez,' it was always just 'Jaci.' "

Born in Houston, Texas, Jaci first displayed her musical gifts before she was two years old. As the congregation sang "Our God Reigns," her father, David Velásquez, the pastor of their church, heard something unusual. He motioned for the congregation to be quiet and soon everyone in the church turned to hear Jaci singing loudly from the nursery. After being "discovered" in a Baptist church in Houston when she was fourteen, Jaci soon moved to Nashville and signed her first record deal.

Being a singer was not something that Jaci consciously decided to do but something that was a natural extension of what she loved to do. "My family was always involved in music and I sang in the church as long as I can remember. I never said, 'I want to be a singer one day.' When I started singing, I was too young to really know what I wanted to be; it just happened to be what I loved to do and I became successful at it, so I continued doing it. I feel blessed that my mother understood this and encouraged it all along.

"My dad was a pastor, but we were very nontraditional and nondenominational. We didn't consider it a religion; it was more of a way of life, trying to live like Jesus. Dad was the pastor, but Mom was really involved too. She was great and she really took care of a lot of things."

Her father stopped pastoring when Jaci was about six years old and began touring the country as an evangelist, singing and preaching the Word of God. Because his other children had left home, David took his wife and daughter on the road with him, living out of their RV. "My father said, 'I want my daughter and my wife with me.' I was the only one left in the house because I was the baby of the family. So I went with Mom and Dad and I was home-schooled from that day forward."

When Diana told her daughter that she was divorcing her husband of twenty-four years, Jaci took the news very hard. "That was a really difficult experience because when you're both Daddy's girl and your mom's best friend, it's really hard. You feel bad because you don't like the way this person is treating that person or the way that person is treating this person, but you don't want to take sides.

"I'm not as close as I wanna be to my dad. It's really been a hard thing because I always feel like I'm betraying one or the other and I hate that feeling, so I just try to stay out of it completely.

"My mom was the one that brought balance to the house. My dad is really cool, but he's a lot more conservative than my mom is. One time my dad didn't want me to wear a certain kind of skirt and my mom said, 'Well, you know, I'll just add some lace to the bottom and she'll be fine.' She'd add two inches of lace and suddenly my dad would say it was great. My mom was the mediator."

While divorce is never easy on the children, regardless of their age, the nineteen-year-old Jaci never doubted where she stood with her parents. Upon hearing of the breakup, Jaci made an unusual decision. "When Mom and Dad were splitting up, I didn't want to live there. So I moved out," Jaci says. "But I lived five minutes away from my mother. It's like I live at home." Despite her splintered family and hectic tour and recording schedules, Jaci has found that she is never far from home—home is wherever her mother is.

"I'm actually at my mom's house more than I am at my own. My mom will call me in the morning and say, 'I'm just calling to wake you up. Get up, come over, and have some coffee.' So I go over and have coffee every morning. And she has all the movie channels, so I end up staying in her living room watching movies all day long. And whenever I stay at her house for the night, I sleep with my mom. I'm like, 'Mom, hug me.' "

Jaci has depended on Diana as both a mother and as a friend from the very beginning of her singing career. A former retail clothing buyer, Diana Catherine is a Mexican-American from New Mexico. Raised Catholic, Diana became a Christian singer and married the evangelical minister and musician David Velásquez. Both had children from previous marriages.

The Velásquez family consisted of three boys and three girls. Jaci explains, "My dad has three kids that he had on his own, well, not all on his own, but before he married my mom. My mom also had three kids, with me being one of them. So technically, I'm the only girl that is from both my parents. I'm my mom's only girl. And my mom is very, very loud in saying, 'I'm gonna leave all my jewelry to my daughter.' But the other girls have moms so they have moms leaving them things."

Although she may not have been raised with all of her siblings, Jaci does work with many of them in the course of her career. "My oldest brother works for me, taking care of all my merchandising. And I have a music publishing company with another brother. My brothers have a lot of respect for my mother and it's kinda funny because they don't even realize that they do it, but they always look for women that remind them of my mom. I just go, 'Oh my God, you are sick, man, you are sick!' "

While Jaci may think her mother's signature lessons were strange, they demonstrated that Diana has always instinctually known something about her daughter. Diana had a vision for her daughter and nothing was going to stop it from being fulfilled.

"My mother sees a lot of things I never could see. I used to have this boyfriend when I was seventeen and we were together for a year. We both lived in Nashville, but about halfway through our relationship, he moved to Dixon, which is about forty-five minutes from Nashville. He would always want me to go out there and see him, but my mom wouldn't let me. One day I said, 'Mom, look, he's gonna come pick me up and drive me up to Dixon. He'll have me back on time for my appointment. I'll be back.' And she goes, 'You're not going.' I said, 'Mom, he's already here in Nashville, it's a short drive out to Dixon and I'll be back by seven P.M., it's fine.' She was like, 'No, you're not going.' Finally I say, 'Well I'm gonna go anyway!' Then my mom said something like 'You'll be out of the will of God.' She goes, 'I don't want that. If you disobey me now, you're disobeying Christ and you're supposed to obey Him.' Needless to say, I didn't go. My boyfriend was traveling back to Dixon and he got a flat. Because he got a flat, I wouldn't have made it back for my appointment that night if I had gone with him. So my mom knows this stuff, she has this insight, this sixth sense that sometimes amazes me. Maybe the second I get pregnant I'll have it too, but I doubt it. I definitely don't have it now.

"My mother was very much the disciplinarian, since Dad was never really around because he was traveling so much. If there was sass with my mom, you could be sure there was a smack across the face. Nowadays people see that as child abuse, but not in my family. You got it all the time." With a laugh, Jaci talks about how the combination of being both Latina and religious is like a discipline

Jaci Velásquez and her mother, Diana Catherine Velásquez in Nashville, Tennessee.

double whammy. "It's over the top. They'll say, 'Because the Bible says so.' Oh my goodness.

"But I respect my mother for not putting up with any of our bullcrap. She never did. Mom never put up with anything and I love and respect her for that. Because if she had, I think we would have grown up differently. I don't want to put up with anything. I think there's a certain balance. Mom was really good at listening to us and not always giving advice. A lot of people think that when people talk to them that they have to have the right words to say and give advice, not my mom. She would sometimes listen and not say anything and that's what makes her a good friend and a good mom. When you can talk to people about everything and they don't always have something to throw back at you, that's what makes up a good friendship. They give advice when you ask for advice.

"I wanna be the kind of mom that mine is—very strong. The kind of mom that doesn't shed tears in front of her kids, but turns around and walks away after spanking them and starts crying afterwards. I truly believed my mother when she said, 'I'm gonna spank you and it's gonna hurt me more than it hurts you.' I respect that and I love her for that and I want to be like that. I don't want to be one of those mothers that sits back and lets the father do everything. If my kids sass me and Dad's not around, I'm not gonna wait till their dad's home to take care of it."

Diana has proved to be a model for her daughter in more than just discipline. Culturally, she has raised her daughter as she was raised, as a Mexican-American. "My brothers and I were caught in a really weird age and time when we were growing up." Jaci explains, "We were growing up at the time when being Latin in my neighborhood was not popular. It was not 'in' to have a Latin last name and to speak Spanish. So as a kid, Mom and Dad never spoke Spanish to us, not because they didn't want to, but because we wouldn't let them. We would say, 'I don't want to hear that stuff, 'cause I have my friends waiting for me outside in the car. So you guys just chill out, you know?'

"But now when I turned about eighteen, I woke up and I said, 'Oh my gosh, I am missing out on the best part of being a person. So I started learning Spanish and I haven't stopped learning."

Jaci's studies have paid off and she has broken through as an artist in the Spanish language market. Her Spanish-language album, *Mi Corazon*, won Female Pop Album of the Year at the Latin Billboard Awards and a Dove Award for Spanish Language Album of the Year. She has performed sold out shows in the Dominican Republic, Panama, Puerto Rico, and throughout Latin America. And with her in every city and every country is Diana.

"My mom goes to everything I go to. She has traveled with me since I was young. When I was sixteen years old, I couldn't go on the road alone. So Mom's been traveling with me and she's been the one that said to my management, 'I can't have her on the bus traveling with a bunch of people she doesn't know.' She told me, 'I'm gonna be here for you in every way as a mother and as a friend, but I don't want to be your manager. I don't want to control your music or your career in any way. That's why you have a great manager. You don't need me for that.' I respect her a lot for that. Mom is very wise in the way she doesn't manage me. She doesn't try to. I don't think I could handle it if she did.

"She does help me choose the people who represent me, though. My mother's got great instinct; she's got a lot of insight into people. She can see when people are not trustworthy and she protects me from that. My mom understands I'm twenty-one years old and that I can make my own decisions. Sometimes she'll come to me and say, 'Hey, do you want to do this? Your manager keeps calling me and saying this is really important, but I told him I need to talk to you first.' She's kind of like the mediator between my manager and me because if I had to deal with everything, I would have no personal life."

While Diana watches out for her daughter in the shark-infested waters of the music world, she also realizes that her daughter is still a young woman facing all the same issues and problems that most young women face. "Mom takes care of so many of the personal and business things.

"I trust my mom with everything and she knows everything about me. She knows the boys I've dated and how many boys I've kissed. She might get upset with or ticked off at me, but she doesn't judge. She is truly a blessing to me." ∎

Life Lessons

Sharo Jimenez

AND HER MOTHER,

Olga Peña

As senior research assistant for the Nickelodeon series *Dora the Explorer*, Sharo Jimenez is very conscious of the importance of images, both in the media and in her personal life. While Sharo's job has her interviewing children about how they feel about the cartoon *Dora*, she has the opportunity to reflect back on the development of her own self-image. ■ Despite all of the contradictory self-image messages that Sharo has had to juggle, she has found that her mother, Olga Peña, continues to show her the most powerful example to follow: her own life.

THE FAMILY DINNERS were the center of Sharo Jimenez's universe as a child. It was there that Sharo found love. It was there that Sharo would join her mother, grandmother, aunts, and female cousins to make dinner in her grandmother's apartment. Although Sharo was born and raised in Providence, Rhode Island, every Sunday she would find herself in New York City's Washington Heights neighborhood. Sharo explains, "Sundays, we would all meet at my grandmother's house. My grandmother had thirteen children, ten of them were living in the U.S. and the rest were in the Dominican Republic. Everyone was packed in that little apartment." Her grandmother, Abuela Mamona, would orchestrate the other women, giving instructions to her various daughters. Sharo's mother, Olga, would in turn give instructions to her daughters. Sharo would peel the garlic while others made the *sofrito* for the rice and beans, all the while listening to the women gossip. The rice and beans they made were always perfect.

"I loved those Sunday dinners," Sharo recalls. "I loved to eat." Sharo explains that although the food was delicious, they were not necessarily balanced or low-calorie meals. "My mom used to make lasagna with rice and beans and a salad. Then she would serve you huge portions of them because like many Latino parents they don't know anything about portion control. Sometimes the poor kids were sitting there saying, *'Yo no quiero mas'* [I don't want anymore], and they would say, *'Que coma, te tienes que comer el plato entero'* [You have to eat your whole plate]. It would give them great happiness to see that you finished your plate."

Coming from a family where food equals love has its problems. While young Latinas were expected to cook and eat, they were expected to remain thin. "Growing up I've always dealt with my weight, so I can't go home and have rice and beans. Or if I do, it better be a very small portion.

"My grandmother's goal was to see me skinny and eventually married. She would tell me, 'Sharo, I'm going to die and I'm never going to see you thin.' I remember I gained at least twenty pounds over a summer in Providence because I knew I was going to spend time in the Dominican Republic to visit my family. During that time they didn't have McDonald's in the Dominican Republic or any other Americanized food. So I said, 'Let me stock up on as much as I can because they are not going to have this there. As soon as I arrived in the Dominican Republic, the first thing my grandmother did was take me to a weight doctor, to a nutritionist. His office was the most degrading thing. There were naked, fat people plastered all over his wall so you could see what you might look like if you kept eating. I was put on a starvation diet. My grandmother would dish out her money like there was no tomorrow to see me skinny."

As much as weight was an issue for Sharo's grandmother, Sharo got a very different message from her mother. "Once she saw me starting to lose weight, she would say, *'Está un poco amarilla, cuidado si tienes anemia'* [You look a little yellow, maybe you're anemic]. She'd say, 'I hope you're not starving yourself.' My mother just wanted me to be happy. She knew I was fat and everyone in my family would make it a point to bring it to her attention, but she never made a big deal about it.

"I had a cousin that would always tell my mother that I was fat because she didn't know how to take care of me. Now she has a daughter who is a little overweight and she doesn't like it when people say her daughter is overweight. I want to say to her, 'Think about the hell that I went through when you would tell my mother in front of me that it's her fault that I'm fat.'

"I was thin right up to the age of nine, but once I hit nine and a half or ten, I just exploded. When I see the pictures, I think, 'Is this the same person?' I guess my brother was maturing and eating more and I was always close to my brother. So while he was having his two sandwiches of scrambled eggs and ketchup, I was alongside him, eating what he was eating." The problem was that because he was older, he was outside playing handball and basketball and doing all these activities while I was inside playing with my dolls."

Every Easter, the Jimenez family would all gather together after church to take a picture of the grandchildren in their new Easter clothes. Sharo remembers one particular Easter when she insisted on not being a part of the photograph.

"I didn't feel pretty and my clothes made me look like an old lady," Sharo recalls. "I never really looked girlish because there was nothing girlish that would fit my size. I remember my sister and my two cousins had the prettiest dresses that Easter. I was ten or eleven and I had a grown-up dress on. I thought my hair was frizzy and ugly and their hair was straight and pretty. My uncles would say, 'Come on, little girls, let's all gather for a picture.' And they all sat on this couch. I looked at myself one more time and all I could do was run to my uncle's room. I locked myself in that room for the rest of the day and cried. I asked God, 'Why, why couldn't I be pretty?' They were all beautiful, light girls with the nice hair and I kept looking at myself thinking I was the only dark girl in the group. I remember asking, 'God, why is it this way?'"

Sharo has spent a lot of time trying to understand why she felt that way and what role her mother played or did not play in helping her understand her feelings. "I never saw myself as pretty and no one ever made me feel like I was pretty in my family. I was always the good one. They would say things to me like, *'Tan Buena que eres'* [You are so good], but never like, *'Que Linda te ves'* or *'que Linda eres'* [You are so pretty]. My sister was the pretty one. She's the one that used to get the compliments.

"I used to be terrified to go to family reunions because I knew people would talk about me because I was still fat or because I had gained weight. I'm such a family person and I love to see my family and bond with them. But once I asked myself, 'Is it worth me coming out of this reunion or this party crying because they are going to say something wrong and intimidate me?' I didn't want to hear them talk about my weight. I haven't gone back to the Dominican Republic in a long time for that reason."

Family has always been very important to Sharo's mother. Olga was born in a small countryside village outside of Moca, Dominican Republic. She grew up in a little hilltop community that was green, lush, and overlooked a beautiful vista. Olga loved her home and it was there that she met her future husband. The couple married and were eventually convinced to leave the Dominican Republic for the supposedly greener pastures of Providence. It was there that they raised their five children. Olga has always instilled in her daughter a sense of pride about being Dominican. This sense of pride is lived out in the culture, the language, and the food.

Those Sunday afternoon dinners were also a learning ground for male and female roles in Sharo's family. Sharo remembers seeing how the women and men behaved differently. "My uncles' wives were so into pleasing them. The guys would be playing cards and dominoes and the women would play bingo, take care of the kids, and cook up a storm. The guys were chilling, listening to their music, telling stories, and playing their games and the women would go up a couple of flights of stairs to take the men their food before they do anything. The women would stop whatever they are doing and serve the men their food." When Sharo pointed out the unfairness of what is expected of the women, her cousin told her, "Sharo, don't you understand that this is how they feel valued? They enjoy doing this, they feel like they are providing for their husbands." But Sharo made it clear that she couldn't do that.

Although Olga quit school after the eighth grade, it was very important to her that her daughter attend college. "While we were growing up, we all knew we were going to college. We didn't know how we were going to get there or how we would pay for it, but we were definitely going.

"My mother was always proud of me. When we had rehearsal for my high school graduation, it wasn't even our graduation day, she just appeared with flowers and bum-rushed the door. She was so happy. I said, 'Mom, what are you doing? This is just rehearsal.' She said, 'I know, but you made it and it's only a couple of days from graduation and I couldn't wait.' She was very excited. Any accomplishment I had was a huge deal for her. For her, it's her own accomplishment because she never had that.

"My parents were really keen on education. It was really important to them that you became something. My mom always wanted the five of us to be successful in life. She would always tell us, 'Whatever I didn't have, I want one of you to have. I want you to be able to provide for your children. I don't want your children to struggle like I had to struggle.' "

Once Sharo entered college, she moved out of her mother's home and into a college dorm. Because her college was only fifteen minutes away from home, Sharo doesn't feel it was much of an independent move. "Even though I was minutes away from home by car, it was hard for my mother to accept that I was living away from home. I had nights where she would call me and say, 'Are they feeding you?' Then she would come over with rice and beans."

Having divorced Sharo's father, Olga has not only had to learn to become self-sufficient but also taught this important lesson to her daughter. "My mother is a big saver and she had to be. There wasn't always money for a new pair of designer sneakers, but she definitely did provide for us. We would never lack food or clothing. We may not have had what we wanted, but we had what we needed.

"For a while, we were on welfare and I was really relieved and happy when my mother got out of it. She was fortunate to get a job, but those jobs are so intimidating. I remember I got a summer job with her in a factory or something. And the guy, yes it was a Caucasian guy, he was just so bad to all of the employees. He talked down to them and I was like, 'How can you stand for this?' I quit that day. I asked her how she could stand to have him talk so low to her but she said she had to because of the medical insurance. She was finally able to break free when she got a job where she's been working as a housekeeper. She was able to break away from the system and provide for her family."

Somehow, with the limited salary that her mother made, she was still able to help Sharo while she was in college. "I was thrilled that she was able to be there for me when I was in school because those books are expensive. She was able to say, 'Here's a portion of my check for you to buy that book.' "

Not all of the lessons Olga taught her daughter were intentional. When it came to love and relationships, Sharo drew her own conclusions by observing her parents' relationship and breakup. "There is love between my mother and the kids, but I never really thought it existed between my parents. When they separated, I tried to look back to find where they might have fallen out of love and I came to the conclusion that they were never in love. I think that when they were dating, it was expected that they would just get married. So, they married and started having children and that's it.

"One Valentine's Day when I was about ten years old, I saw my father give my mother a box of chocolates and flowers. That was the first time that I ever recall him giving her anything for Valentine's Day. My mother kept that heart box for years and it was such a big deal to me. That's when I thought there was love between them because he actually came home with the box of chocolates and flowers for her. My mother would always give him little gifts for his birthday but I don't recall him ever giving her anything until that one time. They would hug when they were in social events but they really never showed their affection in public that much."

Despite Olga's divorce, Sharo sees how her mother emerged from the breakup a changed and stronger woman. "Her big accomplishment after the divorce was getting her driver's license. It was a really big deal for her. After all those years of taking five children on the bus, she just decided to learn how to drive and she did it. She became more independent and outgoing and decided to do things to better herself."

Olga's accomplishments did not end there. She also became a U.S. citizen. "I saw this woman, who didn't speak English, sitting with her lamp and studying every night to become an American citizen. And the teachers were so supportive and so nice to her. I would walk in and she would be so proud of me, saying, 'This is my daughter,' and they would say, 'Oh, we've heard so much about you. Your mom is wonderful.' I was so proud of her and happy that she was getting all this good feedback from the teachers."

Despite all that Sharo has had to sort through in her life, she is beginning to push past a lot of the issues that stood in her way as a child. "I'm still not where I want to be, I still sometimes see myself as fat Sharo. But I know that I've gone far and I walk with more of a bounce when I walk. I'm more proud of myself and I hold my head up higher as I'm walking." And she considers her mother her role model. "It took a strong, resourceful woman to be able to raise five children while making less money than I'm making now. To this day, if I were to give her a call and say I needed something, she would be there for me. I wish someone had told her, 'You are worth it, you are smart enough, you can do this.' She would have gone far. But the fact that she was able to raise us the way she did and have us turn out the way we did is a success story. My mother's success story is us: her children." ■

Sharo Jimenez reclines on her mother, Olga Peña, in New York City's Central Park.

You'll Never Walk Alone

Elizabeth Velez-Velasco

AND HER MOTHER,

Anna Elba Rosario

Elizabeth Velez-Velasco was born and raised on the Lower East Side of New York City with a large family of brothers, sisters, parents, aunts, uncles, and grandparents. While her family seemed to constrain her with responsibilities and expectations as a young girl, it is this same family that she leans on as she battles the AIDS virus. Elizabeth fights not only for her own health but the health of others as she has become active in AIDS awareness, speaking to school groups and attending the AIDS quilt rally in Washington, D.C. ■ Coming to her daughter's defense with unwavering support is Anna Elba Rosario. No stranger to struggle, Anna has joined forces with her daughter to face whatever the future holds for their family.

ELIZABETH IS LIKE HER MOTHER in many ways. Like her mom, her first husband was a man eighteen years her senior. "Love makes you deaf, dumb, blind, and stupid," Elizabeth says. "I met him when I was sixteen. I really didn't like him much, to tell you the truth, because he was too pushy. But I kept seeing him anyway. We kind of lived together when I was about eighteen. Then when I was twenty I had my first child." Elizabeth's mother, Anna Elba Rosario, was not too happy about Elizabeth's choice for a husband because he was too old.

" 'Dios mio!' was the first thing she said when I told her I was moving in with him." Elizabeth describes her mother as a "feisty little thing who doesn't care how old you are, if she has to knock you one, she will." Anna took charge and pulled her daughter's boyfriend into another room to speak to him. Elizabeth says, "I remember him coming out very pale, so I think she kind of threatened him. And then she sat down and really spoke to me. She told me she was cool with me being with him, but 'Don't let no man ever hit you. Your father never hit you, so nobody hits you. If he does, you let us know.' She was very protective, she really was. She's a tough old bird."

In addition to being tough, Elizabeth describes her mother as a woman who enjoys being feminine and dressing up. "She's pretty young-looking and she always dresses up. She does the whole nine yards: the nails, the hair, and the makeup. She's also got that cosmetic tattoo thing going. Her eyebrows, eyeliner, eyeshadow, and lip pencil are all tattooed. She doesn't need makeup when she wakes up; she already looks good. She looks better than I do.

"She also has three tears tattooed on her face. My mom told me the tears are for my grandma and my two brothers who died. I said, 'Mom, that means you killed three people, and she's like, 'Ay, Dios mio!' because she had no idea that's something gang members do. What was she thinking? The only gang she has is us."

When it was time for Elizabeth to get her own apartment, Anna made certain her oldest daughter was close by. "As a matter of fact, my first apartment was right next to hers, she got it for me," recalls Elizabeth. "When I had my first son, Victor, if he was colicky or driving me crazy and I wanted to throw him out a window or something, I would just knock on the wall and she would come right over and scoop him up and let me sleep. She was so cool. As a matter of fact, she was there when Victor was born. When I was ready to go to the hospital, I said, 'Mom, I'm having contractions.' Her shoes were right there but she couldn't find them. So I just said, 'I'll be right back,' and I just took my bag and I made it to Beth Israel hospital by myself.

"When she finally found her shoes, she got there and she was there all the way. When I had my son, that was the first time I really saw my mom cry since my grandma died. I said, 'Mom, I am so sorry for the pain I caused you as a child.' She just started crying and I remember that she said she would pay them to drug me 'cause she couldn't stand to see me crying in such pain. I told her, 'Don't worry, it's something we all have to go through.' "

Anna Elba Rosario was born in Puerto Rico and moved to the United States when she was eight years old. The youngest of seven children, Anna's parents thought that she would have a better life living with her siblings in the States than with them in Puerto Rico. After spending a number of years in Chicago with one sister, Anna left the city to live with another sister in New York.

Anna stayed with her sister until she married. Elizabeth explains, "My pops was an older guy and when my dad saw my mom, he was like, 'Oh, she was it.' Apparently my mom was very, very thin. She had long hair and she was the bomb. She lied. She told him that she was eighteen but she was sixteen and my dad was in his late twenties. I guess she thought she would be better off with my dad than staying with her sister."

Anna's decision to marry a much older man established a pattern that her daughter would follow. Just as Anna disapproved of Elizabeth's marriage, Anna's family wasn't happy about her decision, but Anna was in love and determined. "When I was young, my grandma made it a point to tell me that she did not like my dad at all. But my mom said, 'I love him.' Love is deaf, dumb, blind, and stupid."

Elizabeth discovered that her grandmother's words would come back to haunt her. When her first husband didn't make it to the hospital for the birth of his son, she shrugged off his absence and insisted that they were merely growing apart. "Because the older I got, he got that much older."

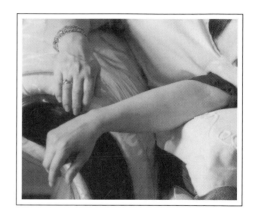

The distance that had been growing in their relationship soon became insurmountable and the couple parted ways.

Elizabeth married a second time and gave birth to her fourth child, a daughter. While life appeared to be improving for Elizabeth and her family, she was dealt a stunning blow in August 1992. Her second husband was diagnosed with AIDS.

"One of my brothers used to use drugs every now and then and he got AIDS. Before he died, his wife, my mom, and I would take turns going to the hospital to be with him and I learned a lot of things. I used to bathe him and take care of him, so I just noticed some things when my husband got ill. He had some qualities and some symptoms that were similar to my brother.

"So I took him to the VA hospital. The doctor was really cool and he asked, 'Would you like for your husband to get tested for AIDS?'

And I said yes. Something told me to get it done. It's kind of like you know, but you don't know.

"They admitted him into the hospital. He didn't want to go because he was just stubborn. But he was really sick. And that was when they took the test. It took two weeks to get the results from that test."

When Elizabeth went to visit her husband one evening, she ran into his doctor who asked her, 'Did you speak to your husband?' And she said, "Why? I haven't been in the room yet," and he said, "Well, I'll give you some time to speak to your husband. Then I need to speak to you." Elizabeth waited for what seemed to be an interminable period of time. "When I finally go see my husband, he says nothing, all he does is cry. So then I go back to the doctor and he tells me my husband has AIDS and that I should get tested too.

"The first person I went to was my dad and he said, 'Oh, you don't have it.' But my mom said, 'Just get tested and you're gonna be fine.' The period following Elizabeth finding out that her husband had AIDS now seems like a big blur to her. She remembers going to get tested, then thinking that she had to get her youngest daughter tested. "I had to get my girl tested because she was the last to come into this world. Two weeks later, when the results were in I went in to see my doctor, who said, 'I have good news and bad news.' I said, 'All right, give me the bad news.' He asked, 'You don't want the good news?' and I told him to give me the bad news. He said, 'I'm sorry, but you have the HIV virus.' Then I asked about my daughter and he said, 'The good news is the girl doesn't have it.' And that's all I heard because I got on my knees and I said, 'Thank you, Lord. You are merciful, for You have spared my daughter.' All I could think about was that for me it was okay, I would figure out a way to deal, but you don't want your children to be sick."

According to a 2000 report from the Centers for Disease Control and Prevention (CDC), in 1986 Latinas accounted for more than twenty percent of AIDS cases in women. By

Elizabeth Velez-Velasco reclines on her mother, Anna Elba Rosario.

1995, Latinas were seven times more likely than were white women to contract the HIV virus. A 1999 report by the CDC stated that although Latina and African-American women together comprise less than twenty-five percent of all women in the United States, they make up seventy-seven percent of AIDS cases to date.

The 1999 CDC report states that most women generally contract the HIV virus from having sexual intercourse with a man who has been infected, usually through intravenous drug use.

"When I found out I was ill, I couldn't see my husband for two weeks, because I really wanted to hurt him. I really, really wanted to hurt him and then I started seeing a counselor and I started understanding. I had to sit down and explain to the family and explain to the kids what was going on. They thought I was gonna die within a week or something like that, so they took it really bad. But they were little kids then. Now my son says, 'You're not dying, you're not gonna die, you're gonna haunt us forever.'

"My mom didn't take it well. I felt so bad because she cursed God, which is not cool, because He had nothing to do with it. She got very upset, she was thinking of all the things that she could do, like she could take out a contract on my husband or something like that. I said, 'Mom, I'm gonna be okay.' When my brother died, the only drug they had was AZT, but there are so many other drugs now. I was always up to date on information about new medicines and I'm still here, praise God. God and I, we have this thing. I always say we have this thing, He and I, and He can take me now if He wants. I'm ready, it's okay. But He knows that I'll be more than happy to leave this world as soon as my youngest daughter Olivia is eighteen and in college. Then I'm cool. Then it's like 'I'm coming.' "

When it comes to her children dealing with her illness, Elizabeth tries to give them constant positive reinforcement. By using her life as an example, Elizabeth and her daughters participate in many AIDS awareness conferences and try to disseminate information about the devastating effects that AIDS is causing, particularly in the Latino community. Most important, Elizabeth wants her daughters to live and cherish the present. "I want my daughters to be real, to be in the here and now and not to live in the past. I want them to be real and to cherish each day. Every day is a new day, don't look back on yesterday because it's not gonna happen again and just see what you're going to do today and look forward to tomorrow, good, bad, or indifferent."

Naturally, the news of her condition has affected her relationship with everyone, but especially with her mother. "We try to spend a lot of time together. I see her at least once a week and we call each other a lot. I'll call one day, then she'll call the next. If we don't hear from each other she gets paranoid.

"I tell my mother that when I die, I want to have a big party, because every Thanksgiving, every Christmas, or every holiday, I used to throw big parties for my family. That's what I'm most famous for in my family—baking and the cooking. So I want my family to throw a party, throw some salsa on and have a good time. I mean it's only my body's leaving, my spirit lives on. I just I think it's just another step. I want my ashes to be thrown somewhere in the Caribbean because I really need to get a tan." ∎

Laughter and Tears

Janice Garcia

AND HER MOTHER,

Nelly Awilda Garcia Sainz

Born in Santurce, Puerto Rico, Janice Garcia grew up on army bases all over the American South and Southwest. As a stand-up comic, Janice has made a considerable splash as the announcer on the popular syndicated series *It's Showtime at the Apollo.* She has also appeared on HBO's *The Chris Rock Show* and has a one-woman show called *15 Minutes of Fem.* ■ Janice's mother, Nelly Awilda Garcia Sainz, is very much a performer in her own right. Formerly a professional belly dancer, Nelly passed her love of the limelight on to her daughter. Together, both women have learned to overcome the often challenging events of their tumultuous lives with a healthy dose of comedy.

WHEN COMEDIAN Janice Garcia takes the stage to perform her comic routine, the character she most enjoys playing is that of her mother. Laughing, Janice says, "I do my mom and I do all of her mannerisms. I'm surprised when people laugh. I wonder what they're laughing at sometimes, but since comedy is about relating to people, if they laugh, they relate."

When Janice writes the material for her stand-up, her comedy comes from the important events and people in her life. So it is telling that her favorite subject is her mother. "I use real conversations I have with her. Lately I'm working on a routine where she's obsessed with weight loss and she's trying these meditational tapes. I'll ask her, 'How much did you pay for these?' and she'll say, 'I'm not going to tell you. Don't bother me, they are my tapes. I paid for them, all right. It's my money.' "

One of Janice's earliest memories is of a birthday cake her mom made for her fourth birthday. The cake was custom-made in the shape of a swimming pool. Janice recalls, "She took coconut shavings and colored them green to make them into grass. In the center of the grass was a pool with real water and real goldfish. When she was transferring the goldfish from the bag to the pool, one of the fish fell down the sink and I cried. She tried to console me, but all I remember is that fish going down the sink."

Another memory that has haunted Janice is the time her grandmother told her she was born out of wedlock. Janice says, "My grandmother asked me if I ever wondered why my parents don't have wedding pictures. I'm a child so I say, 'I don't know.' And she says, 'Because your parents had you out of wedlock and that's a sin.' I mean, I heard years of this."

Subsequently, Janice heard the story of how her parents met in college in Puerto Rico. With two more years of college, her mother, Nelly, discovered that she was pregnant and that forever changed their family. Nelly's mother insisted that she finish school and that during those two years she would raise her daughter's child.

"My grandmother mostly raised me," Janice recalls. "She kind of just grabbed me. And she was very possessive about it because she would not let me go to my father's mother. She wanted me with her. I remember her telling me, 'I'm your *abuela*, I'm Mami. That is Mercedes.' 'Til this day I call my father's mother Mercedes, by her name. I don't call her Mami or Abuela and that's because of my mother's mother. I called my mother Mamá.

"I feel like you absorb things as a

child and those are your years where you are really impressed upon. I know that I just have a lot of phobias and the Catholic guilt. It's in me and I feel like my grandmother put that in there.

"My grandmother is this powerful and intimidating woman. I think everybody either feared her or just didn't want to deal with her. And she has pushed everybody away. Now she's alone. My grandfather died and she's alone in Puerto Rico. My mother tries to build up the courage to call her, but then she breaks out into hives."

Janice's grandmother, like Janice, was born out of wedlock. Janice says, "My grandmother won't talk about it. I want to do my family tree. I want to go back, because my grandmother didn't know her father. My mom said he was a sailor. He was black. He was dark-skinned. It's weird. We have *una mescla* [a racial mix] and I always wanted to know what it was, but it's frustrating because my grandmother is ashamed. She's still ashamed because they made fun of her when she was a child."

Eventually Janice's grandmother married, began a career as a teacher, and had four children, including Nelly. When it looked to her that her daughter Nelly was going to repeat the same mistake that she made, she put her foot down, with all the weight of Catholicism and Puerto Rican tradition behind her. Janice says, "My mother and her mother have never reconciled because she had me before she was married. It was a sin and my grandmother was like the fear of God, very Catholic. It was traumatizing and they are still dealing with that after all these years."

After Janice was born, her parents married under intense pressure from Janice's grandmother. "I feel like I don't know the whole story, so I'm just making these assumptions that they were forced to get married. You have this child coming into the world now and you have to be married because that's the way Catholic people do it."

Nelly Garcia and her daughter, Janice Garcia, in Los Angeles.

When her parents finished school at the University of Puerto Rico, Nelly retrieved her two-year-old daughter from her mother's care and headed for Kentucky. "Both of my parents were in ROTC in college." Janice recalls, "When my father graduated, he went into the army as an officer and went to pilot school stateside. That was the first time they had me by themselves. They told me that they were nervous because I had been with my grandmother all that time and I had never been with them."

The Garcia family traveled through the Southwest, going from Kentucky to Texas to Alabama, where Janice's sister was born when Janice was four years old. The family continued to travel, spending time on military bases in North Carolina and Puerto Rico. When Janice's father was stationed overseas in Korea and Germany, Nelly decided to keep her family in the States.

Janice remembers those difficult times. "By the time my father got assigned to Germany, my parents were having trouble. Finally my mother moved to an apartment complex five minutes away and we stayed with my father. I still saw her but it was weird. She wasn't living with us."

Janice has conflicted feelings about her parents' separation and about her mother in particular. "I guess I did miss my mom. I don't feel like I had a great relationship with my parents when I was growing up. I felt alone a lot. But at the same time, when she would come to the school, all the kids would be like, 'Is that your mom?' My mom was beautiful. Kids are usually embarrassed to have their parents come pick them up at school, but when my mom came I was like 'Yes, that's my mom.'

"She wore those Diane von Furstenberg wraparound skirts and now that they've come back she's all pissed because she threw them all away. My mom was always together with her clothes. She always looked good."

Looking good was important to Nelly because she was more than just a beautiful mother; she was a professional belly dancer. Janice says, "It's not like ice-skating or basket-ball where you go pro but she was professional because she would go to Atlanta and Boston and take all these seminars and she was really into it. And she performed in really good Greek and Turkish restaurants. I don't know where she got that from. She just always liked it. She was attracted to that whole Middle Eastern thing. She told me that she paid for my college with her belly dancing money in Germany."

While she enjoyed seeing her mother dress up in scarves and bangles, she also realized that she was not like her mother. "I observed my mom but that was not in me. I admired her because I was in awe of how she carried herself, but I was nothing like that. I was this shy little tomboy. I was more into sports. Volleyball, basketball, soccer, I played them all."

Despite the differences Janice perceives between her mother and herself, she remembers her mother making her dress up for school concerts. "I would shout and scream while she dressed me, but when I wore it I was like, 'Yeah.' Then I would go to the school and people would be like, 'Oh my God, look at Janice. You look good.' And I would be all shy, like I'm so embarrassed."

Janice's little sister, however, couldn't have been less like Janice. "My sister came out just like my mom.

She just took her right under her armpit. She imitated my mom and that's how she got into belly dancing. She was imitating her one day and my mom said, 'Hey, you are pretty good.' "

Janice's sister began dancing when she was three years old and became professional at seven. At eight, she made her debut on the popular television series *That's Incredible!* Nelly had sent a video of her baby daughter flipping coins on her stomach to the producers of the show. The Garcia family flew out to Los Angeles for the taping of the show, leaving Janice behind.

Although Janice felt she had little in common with her talented mother and sister, she was shining with her own talents outside of her family's spotlight. "I won a contest for writing a poem about Christmas. I knew I had a creative thing in me, but I was so shy that it didn't come out until my senior year in high school. Because my sister was so up front and in the limelight, and I didn't feel comfortable expressing my creativity to anyone, I just kind of kept it in for a long time. I drew, I played the guitar, I played the bass clarinet, and I played the alto clarinet. I did sports. I think I was just like screaming for attention from them and I did everything."

Finishing her senior year in Germany, Janice took a drama class with an instructor known for being difficult and extremely strict. She recalls, "Everybody was intimidated by him but I went to class and he loved me. He thought I was really talented and that was it. I noticed that he was different with me than he was with everybody else, and I said, 'Okay, I got something here.' My parents were like, 'Oh no, it's just another hobby,' because I had all these hobbies. I just feel like I didn't get the support from them like my sister got."

Eventually, Janice not only took acting classes but she discovered that her passion was comedy. "A big part of me choosing this career is to get the attention that I didn't get as a child. It's like I look for it now on stage. I feel like comedy gives it to me.

"That's how I became this clown with my mom. I was just

the joker. I was the one always trying to make her laugh. Her office was within walking distance from my high school, so on my lunch break I would go over to her office and if she wasn't there, I'd hang Post-it notes with these funny little sayings so that she'd see them when she came back. My way of reaching out was always to make her laugh.

"As I got older I used humor with my mother because I felt like if I made her laugh she would like me. I never felt comfortable doing that for my dad, because he didn't think I was funny. He would be like, 'Stop playing games.' He was always serious with me. So to this day, there are no jokes about my dad in my act because he made me feel like I wasn't funny. My jokes are all about my mom."

Janice's jokes are not only about her mother, they are *for* her mother. Knowing her mother is in the audience gives Janice the freedom to express what would be difficult under different circumstances.

Janice says, "I'm trying to get a little deeper and a little more into the pain and trying to turn the pain around and make it funny, which is really difficult without therapy. In this new routine, I'm dealing with the fact that my mother, like my grandmother, is this dog person. My grandmother was a dog lady and my mom has become a dog lady, too. She has all these little dogs and sometimes I feel like the dogs get better treatment than me.

"Her mom was just like that, too. My grandmother talked about committing suicide and disappearing off the face of the earth. She said that the only reason she doesn't do it is because of her dogs, and until the dogs die she's not going anywhere. I said, 'Fine, I'll just keep bringing you dogs so you can stay alive.' Crazy. The guilt that they throw on you is crazy." ■

With One Voice

Carol Cárdenas

AND HER MOTHER,

Minerva Cárdenas

Carol Cárdenas is better known as Carol C, the voice and force behind Si*Sé. The band's self-titled debut album was described as a "sublime delight" by *Billboard* magazine. After formal training in opera, Carol has used her Dominican and Arabic background to create her own sound. ■ While Minerva Cárdenas was unable to pursue the music career that she desired for herself, both mother and daughter have found satisfaction in watching Carol's dreams come true.

GROWING UP, Carol C and her mother, Minerva Cárdenas, had a ritual—every Saturday morning they would thoroughly clean the house, play loud music, and sing at the top of their lungs. "My mom would blast her Julio Iglesias, Camilo Sesto, and Sandro records because she was big into Spanish ballads," she says, laughing, "Oh my God, she loved how Sandro gyrated his hips." Back then, Carol rejected her mother's musical selections because she preferred disco music. Although she would say, "Mom, change that music!" she now admits that she kind of liked it.

Those were the early years when Carol's mother belonged just to her and they shared a bond that her other brothers and sisters did not. Minerva married Carol's father at twenty-four and had three children in the Dominican Republic. Minerva and her husband decided to come to America in search of a better life for their children. "When my parents first came to America, it was just the two of them. They left my brothers and sisters with other relatives in the Dominican Republic. My parents had decided that they weren't having any more children, but once they moved to New York, I kind of came as a surprise."

Carol was about four years old when her brother and sisters finally joined the family in New York. "Before my brother and sisters arrived, my mom went back and forth to visit them in the Dominican Republic," she recalls. "It was really, really hard on her because she missed them so much. But she felt like she had to do that in order to give them a better life. I think she put so much energy into me because I was

the only child she had here in New York. I became very attached to my mom. Of all the kids, I'm the most attached. And she was also very, very loving to me."

Minerva worked a lot during that time and she didn't have a lot of time for the little things. Carol says, "If I needed help with homework, she couldn't really help me. She was a seamstress and used to design clothing at home. She was super-motivated. She was such a good seamstress that I could draw anything I wanted to wear and she would make exactly what I wanted. She stopped sewing a few years ago because it's really bad for her vision. But if I really wanted her to make something for me she would."

Minerva is the youngest daughter in a family of six brothers and sisters. Her father, who was born in Jerusalem, sailed to Santo Domingo looking for an adventure in a new place. There, he fell in love with Minerva's mother and, though he spoke very little Spanish, decided to stay in the Dominican Republic. Minerva grew up in the Dominican Republic but she was heavily influenced by her father's Arabic culture. "My grandmother learned how to cook Arabic food and she taught my mom how to cook it, so we grew up with Arabic food with rice and beans and *platanos*," Carol reports.

Like Carol, Minerva loved to sing ever since she was a kid. "My mother used to perform with her friends outside after school and even joined a chorus. She wanted to pursue a singing career, but she wasn't allowed to. Because her dad died so young and her mom couldn't raise so many kids alone, her older sister took her in and raised her. Her brother-in-law was pretty strict. He didn't think music was a good career for a young lady, so she was not allowed to pursue it. My mom thought that maybe later on in life she would get a chance to pursue singing on a professional level. Then she married my dad, who was another very conservative man, and he wasn't having it."

Carol believes that is the reason her mother was so invested when Carol first showed an interest in singing at a very young age. "My mom was always saying, 'She's gonna be a singer, watch.' I heard that being reinforced since I was little, and since I loved performing from the time I was four, I knew I was gonna be a singer. I sang in high school and because of my mother, I'm still singing today."

One of Carol's favorite pastimes was putting on shows for her mother. "My sisters and I would get dressed up, put a towel on our heads (pretending to have long, luxurious hair), then perform. My mom was the only audience member." No matter what the Cárdenas girls sang, Minerva would clap and tell them how wonderful and talented they were.

Although Carol was a ham at home, she was very shy when it came to performing in public. "I thought, 'If I could only perform outside the way I perform at home, people would know how good I can sing.' But when I got out there I sounded like Minnie Mouse. My mom would tell me that she didn't like me singing all mousy. She criticized me for being

shy a lot, and she would tell me, 'If you keep singing like that, you're never gonna get on *Sabado Gigante!*'"

When Carol was in the third grade, they used to put on shows every year at her school that always featured one girl soloist. Carol remembers, "The soloist did this cute little dance with an umbrella and she'd dress in a pretty little outfit. I always wanted to be that girl. And so my teacher had us sing that song one time just to hear which of us would be a good singer. When it was my turn to sing, my teacher stood next to me for a while. I was so nervous singing but she said, 'You have a really good voice.' So she talked to my mother and said, 'She has a great voice and I want her to be the soloist for this year's show.'"

Carol and her mother couldn't have been more excited. Unfortunately, the show was canceled that year. "They didn't do it, so of course I didn't get to do the whole little dance with the umbrella. But I think that's when my mom really paid attention to me wanting to be a singer."

Because of her mother's constant encouragement and support, Carol studied opera at the highly competitive LaGuardia High School of Music and Art. "My father was just as conservative with his kids as he was about his wife and he was against my going to the school of performing arts the whole time." It didn't matter

Minerva Cárdenas and her daughter, Carol Cárdenas, in the studio.

that this was a highly regarded school that required a rigorous set of auditions to be accepted. Carol's father was adamant that she go to the same school Carol's sisters went to. "Whenever my mother told him that I wanted to go to La-Guardia, he would say, 'No. She's going to Catholic school.'"

So Minerva took matters into her own hands. "My mom told him that we applied to the Catholic school and that there were no more applications, because that would happen sometimes. She told my father, 'They are not accepting any more kids this year. Next year we'll put her in Catholic school. But she really wants to go to the performing arts school and that's the only one that she got accepted in.' And he accepted it for a year. He said, 'Okay. She can go, but just for one year. That's not a good school. She has to go to Catholic school and learn about religion.' After that year, my mom and I just kept quiet. We never mentioned it. My father was working a lot and he forgot about it.

"Throughout high school, my mom and I had a plan. She would say, 'Okay, you're gonna be a singer, now what can we do?' I even got braces, because she said, 'You have to fix your teeth because you're gonna be in the public a lot.' So I started

working my junior year in high school. Right after school I would run to my job so that I could save money to pay for my braces."

Both Carol and her mother were united in a single vision and purpose. Minerva taught her daughter that together they could accomplish whatever they set out to do. "The most important lesson I learned from my mother is that anyone can do anything they want if they focus, put energy into it, and feel like they can. You can't be wishy-washy about things because then you get a wishy-washy outcome. You have to be like, 'Of course that's what I'm gonna be.' Not only was my mother saying that I was going to be a performer, she had my whole family saying, 'She's definitely gonna be something important because she walks around like it.'

"My mom always told me education is very important, that even though I wanted a career in music, I should still have something to fall back on. Also, college was the only way I could move out of the house. My father would not let me move out of the house until I got married. Marriage or college. My oldest sister picked marriage. She got married very young, she was nineteen. She didn't want to go to college at the time so she just moved out with her husband. I thought, 'Nah, that's not my style.' So I went away to college."

When Carol graduated, she joined a band as a backup singer and toured with a singer called Amber Sunshower. After doing independent work as a singer, a DJ, and a producer, Carol decided that it was time for the next big phase of her career. "I decided I really wanted a band and it was kind of one of those things that just happened. From the minute I had a demo, my mother would call me every few days and go, 'Did you register your songs? You know you have to register them because if someone steals your songs you can't do anything unless it's registered.' I'd be like, 'Where is she getting all that information from?' She's definitely on top of the business side of things.

"She's always taught me to be really positive and not to dwell on negative things. Anytime there was a problem with the band, and we ran into financial problems, she would always be like, 'Okay, this is the problem. How do we solve it?' She wasn't too much of a dweller or a martyr type. She would take money out of the rent if I had a show and I needed a new shirt or something. She would say, 'I'm gonna have to give the rent money in late, but here's the money.' Always us first.

"Even though I'm a super-duper underground performer, to my mom I'm a star. My mom wants to see me and my band tour badly, but we travel in two little vans. She says she doesn't care, that she'll sleep in the van, but I wouldn't put her through that. But my mom has seen me perform at the Apollo. She loved it seeing me perform on a big stage because until then, she'd only seen me in little clubs and lounges. One night when I ran to the front of the stage to give out T-shirts at the end of my set, she was the first person to run up. I was like, 'Mom I can give you one when I get offstage.' But she was like, 'Give one to me!' She's a true fan."

But far more than a fan, she's one of her daughter's best friends. "I think we just keep getting closer and closer as the years go by. I definitely feel closer to her now than I did even last year." Carol hopes to sing a duet with her mother on her next album. Hopefully it will be just like the old days: the music loud and mother and daughter singing at the top of their lungs. ∎

The Beat in My Heart

Lisa Lisa

AND HER MOTHER,

Monserrate Velez

Lisa Marie Velez first burst onto the music scene in 1985 with the dance classic "I Wonder If I Take You Home." Christened as Lisa Lisa, she was the frontwoman for the group Cult Jam and saw a string of hits top the charts, including "Head to Toe," "All Cried Out," and "Lost in Emotion." In addition to singing, Lisa has begun acting and was recently featured in the Nickelodeon series *Taina*. She also maintains an exhaustive, around-the-world touring schedule. ■ Much of Lisa's success is built on the sacrifice of her remarkable mother, Monserrate "Monse" Velez. Monse found she had the strength and drive to do what appeared impossible: raising ten children by herself.

LISA LISA HAS ALWAYS been known to follow her heart's desire. And this time was no different. When her fiancé asked her what she wanted for Valentine's Day last February, she did not hesitate before answering, "I want another tattoo!" She recalls the story with the excitement of a kid who got exactly what she wanted for Christmas. "When I went to get my tattoo, I thought hard about what I was going to get because I wanted it to be special. Then I decided to get my mother's name 'Monse' tattooed right above my butt. When I showed the tattoo to Mami, she said, 'Lisa, why did you do that?' and I said, 'Mami, I dedicated my body to you.' Now she thinks it's funny and makes me show it to all my relatives anytime we get together."

Not every woman would have her mother's name permanently applied to her behind, but Lisa Lisa is no ordinary woman and Monse is no ordinary mother.

Monserrate Lopez was born in Spain but her parents immigrated to Puerto Rico when she was four years old. While she was still quite young, both of her parents died and Monse was raised by her grandmother and aunt in the countryside of Puerto Rico. Many years later, Monse found her way to the big city of New York, with her first husband and two baby girls. The couple had three more children before he died. Lisa recounts, "She had five children with her first husband and then she met my father and had five more kids. They got divorced right before I was born. She had me when she was thirty-six."

After the death of her first husband and the divorce from her second, Monse found herself raising ten children on her own. "I admire the strength that she had because ten kids will put you through some stress. Being single and having to get odd jobs to raise ten kids on your own is really hard. But I saw my mom work through all this."

The Velez family of eleven lived in three bedrooms. The baby of the family, Lisa watched while her mother earned money by baby-sitting and selling big pots of rice and beans to her neighbors in Hell's Kitchen. Lisa remembers, "She made *pasteles* for the holidays and sold them to everybody in the building. But most of the time she gave everything out for free. Sometimes people had to force her to accept the money for her food. Remember the government cheese? Well there were so many of us that sometimes we would go on the line twice and then sell the cheese to the grocery stores to make a little cash on the side and give it to Mom. We would say, 'Here, Mami, we made ten dollars for you today,' and she would be so happy.

"That lady taught me well. I grew up seeing that if she had one egg she would cook that egg and would split it for all ten of us. She always told us to share whatever you have with those you love because one day you're gonna need them too. Sometimes, I would watch her sit there for twenty minutes and cry because she was trying to figure out how she was going to take care of all of us. That's the only time Mami would hide herself in her room. She never hid anything from us except when she was scared that she would do something wrong. What mother is not going to be scared to do something wrong in raising her child? Just knowing that she would sit there and think about how she was going to feed us that day is what makes me get up every morning and say, 'I got to move on.' That is the strength, that is the power that she implanted within me."

It is that strength that Lisa relied on when she was nine years old and got the opportunity to sing "Ave Maria" in her Catholic church. "I loved to sing," Lisa remembers. "When I sang the 'Ave Maria,' I remember watching my mother and singing to her. I thought, 'I'm not gonna get nervous. I'm just gonna look at my mother and I'm going to sing to her.' And she was crying, and I whispered, 'Ma,' and she said, 'Shhh, sing.' So I continued to sing while she continued to cry. It was hard but she loved it. After that I thought, 'Gee, I had a really big effect on her.'"

Lisa soon discovered that her voice had a big effect on everyone who heard her. When she was thirteen, she would sneak out of her mother's house and go to the clubs that were scattered along Forty-sixth Street in Manhattan. "One day I snuck out and went to Fun House, a club near my house, because they said that's where Madonna got discovered. I said if she could get discovered there so can I. And that is where I met Mike Hughes of Cult Jam."

He told Lisa that he was auditioning girls to form a three-girl group the following Thursday. Thinking that was the chance of a lifetime, she took the train to Brooklyn and went to the audition after school. There were so many girls there

that she waited until eleven-thirty at night before it was her turn to perform. "I knew my mother was going to kill me because I went there without permission. I thought to myself, 'If I call my mother now she's gonna send somebody to come get me.' So I just stood there and didn't call."

When it was her turn to sing, the producers handed her a new song to learn called "I Wonder If I Take You Home." It would later become the first hit of the yet-to-be-formed eighties supergroup, Lisa Lisa and Cult Jam. But that was in the future. In Lisa's immediate present was an angry mother. "When I got home I think it was around one o'clock in the morning and my mother had called the cops. The cops were standing in the kitchen when I walked in. As soon as I walked through the door, she slapped me and said, 'You don't understand what you did to me.' I said, 'Mami, I'm sorry,' and I told her the whole story. She said, 'Don't ever do that again!' All I could say is, 'All right, I'm sorry.'"

A few days later, Lisa recorded her first two songs and shortly thereafter was signed to a recording contract. "I didn't even know I was going to get the contract," Lisa confesses. "I thought, I'm still in school and Mami's not going to let me do this. So I had to ask my mother if it was okay and she went through this whole drama after that. She said she didn't know whether or not she was going to let me sign the contract or go on tour. But after I graduated and I received my diploma, my mother let me go—but only if I took my older brother with me."

Monse should not have been surprised to find that her daughter was interested in singing. As it happens, singing was a joy that both mother and daughter shared.

Lisa recalls her mother telling her about how she used to sing at every opportunity. "She used to sing with *parandas* and all that. She would be cooking and she sang. She would be washing dishes and she sang. She would be changing our diapers and she would sing. She sang everything from Spanish songs to Tom Jones. I remember she would be watching the Tom Jones show on TV and she would take pictures of the TV. I asked her, 'What the hell are you doing?' I would laugh because since she didn't speak English, she wouldn't know what he was saying. She would be singing Tom Jones songs and I would ask her, 'What are you singing?' She would say, 'I don't know, but I'm singing.'

"My mom has a beautiful voice and I think she could've been a professional singer. I really do believe she would've been an entertainer because she has that mouth for music."

While Monse wasn't able to pass on to her daughter formal training in music, she certainly was able to pass on practical advice that served Lisa well as a young girl constantly on the road without her mother.

Lisa would call her mother from everywhere she traveled just to feel reassured. "I could have a bad dream and wake up at three o'clock in the morning and call my mother and say, 'Mami, what should I do?' She would say, 'Relax, just write it down and when you get up in the morning, you'll realize what it means.' Everything she ever said to me stayed with me even when she was not around. Even today those words ring in my ear. That's why at the end of the day before I shut my eyes to go to sleep, I have to make that phone call to her. I have to hear her say 'I love you,'

Lisa Lisa in her Times Square neighborhood.

because then I know everything is all right."

Monse has always told her children to turn to her when they had problems or questions. And Lisa took her mother at her word. "She told each and every one of us, 'Whenever you are going to "do the do," tell me. Don't be afraid.' She never stopped us from watching certain things or reading certain books. She would say, 'I want you to learn, but when you have that thing in your head and that little itch between your legs, you come over here and you ask me because I'm going to tell you exactly what you want to know.'

"And here it was. Finally, my day to 'do the do.' I was almost nineteen, I was already on tour and doing all this stuff. I didn't know about sex, but I'm singing about sex. I told my mom, 'Ma, I'm gonna go hang out.' I went over to this guy's house and we hung out and we did the nasty. An hour after, I said to him, 'I gotta go, I gotta go.' He's like, 'Damn, was I not as good as I said?' So I got up, got on that bus and I went home. I was crying because I was nervous. I went home and I took a shower and when I jumped out of the shower my mother saw that something was wrong with me. I said, 'Don't be mad at me. I did it.' She was like, '*Carajo!* What did you do? What did you do?!' She's thinking something really bad happened and I was gonna go to jail. I said, 'I had sex.' And she broke out into this laughter. I said, 'Why are you laughing at me?' She goes, ''Cause I didn't think you were gonna tell me. Lisa, I swear you are the only one out of my ten children that ever told me.'

"I was the only ass to tell her I lost my virginity. It was the topic of conversation in my family for the next month because my mother called everybody, even in Puerto Rico to tell them 'Lisa lost her virginity.' They were all congratulating me because I waited so long. It was just not normal. They thought in a Latin family for this little Puerto Rican hottie that's on the stage every day to wait this long was just not normal. So after that everything and anything about sex, I talk about with my mother."

As difficult as her circumstances in life may have been, Monse has not let it make her bitter. As long as she had her children around her, there was nothing to be bitter about. Lisa explains, "She never seemed unhappy about things. Like when she got rid of my father, she devoted herself to raising her kids and making herself happy. She loved her first husband wholeheartedly. She loved her second husband, who was my father, but she knew she had to get rid of him because love shouldn't hurt. Mami said, 'My kids come first.' That's one thing my mother told me: when you decide to have children you don't live for yourself anymore, it's about your kids. That's what she's taught me about love.

"I saw my mother being happy doing things with the family, like making rice and beans and feeding us. Family makes Mami happy. She loves that. My mother loved herself and loved her kids enough to choose us. She never had boyfriends after her second husband. I never asked her why, but she never seemed unhappy about it. She had ten great kids. That's a success story because she did it all by herself."

Lisa's mother was recently diagnosed with Alzheimer's disease and both mother and daughter are going through difficult periods dealing with the illness. "I love my mother to death," Lisa says. "She's my pride and joy and that's why I wanted a full tattoo of her name on my body. She makes me smile. The sun, the smile, and the moon, it is here." ■

It Takes a Village

Nora Lago

AND HER MOTHER,

Carmen Lago

Nora Lago has both an unusual career and an unusual history. Nora has overcome many obstacles to become an accomplished holographer. While her relationship with her mother is strong and loving, it has been complicated by her parents' drug abuse and their subsequent abandonment of her in an unconventional drug rehabilitation program. ■ Carmen Lago has not only survived breast cancer and a difficult life, but has emerged stronger—a benefit shared by both mother and daughter.

"I WAS A MISTAKE when I was born," says Nora when asked about her childhood. For most of her life, Nora believed she was born an addict. And why wouldn't she? Both her father and mother were addicted to heroin. Nora's mother was using heroin so heavily during her pregnancy that about a month before delivery it caused serious health complications. Nora recounts the story that's been passed down to her. "She started having heart palpitations. They kept my mother at Bellevue Hospital until I was born."

However, less than a year later, drugs again took over Carmen's life. Nora's parents admitted themselves into a drug detox facility in a Lexington, Kentucky prison. Because Nora's grandparents were unable to take care of the infant Nora, her parents placed her in a convent in Long Island, where she remained until she was three. During this time, Nora's father was admitted to Synanon, a radical and controversial drug rehabilitation program in California.

Charles Dederich created Synanon in 1958 as a drug rehabilitation program. Developed in Ocean Park, California, the program was based on the premise that only former addicts can successfully help other addicts recover. Synanon (which is derived from Sins Anonymous) is far more than a rehab program, however. By the 1970s, Synanon declared itself to be a church and fashioned itself as a utopian society for people looking for countercultural enlightenment.

For those addicts struggling with recovery, this enlightenment was accomplished through group sessions of verbal and mental abuse (called The Game). Nora's father discovered that the brutal approach worked for him and he thought it could work for Carmen as well. He sent for Carmen and Nora. Nora would remain in the quasireligious society for the next sixteen years.

"At first, I lived in a beautiful house with my mother and father, and then the administrators of the program decided to separate parents from their kids, placing all of the kids in dorms."

Many commonly held views of family were thrown out of the window. The routine Synanon practice of separating children from their parents was particularly difficult for Carmen, who had to break from her traditionally held Latin views of what it meant to be a mother. As time passed, however, Carmen found herself adopting a new belief system.

Not long after she moved into the dormitory, her mother fell in love with a man she met in the program.

"There's a lot that led up to that. My father wasn't paying attention to my mom because he was too busy being a big shot there. She needed some affection. She and this Puerto Rican guy, Louie, ended up getting together and leaving Synanon. They went to live in a hotel nearby. My father sent me to Yosemite National Forest for two weeks because he found out that my mom was going to leave and take me with her. When I came back my mom was gone.

"I couldn't believe that she didn't say good-bye. I couldn't believe she didn't take me with her. I remember waiting up for her at night. I would fall asleep by the door because I knew she was coming back for me. I waited for a year until one morning I realized she wasn't coming back. My father didn't want her to have any contact with me at all. I hated my father at that time. Any letters or phone calls from my mother were intercepted. That was my father's doing.

"They literally had a guard at my dormitory and I didn't know about it. If anyone were to see my mother on the premises, they would call the police. I found out later that three residents went to the hotel she was staying at and told my mother that if she didn't get out of there within two days, they were going to break her legs. They put a lot of fear in her and that's why she took off to New York without me.

"I found out what happened when I was sixteen or seventeen by listening to some tapes. I was going through the Synanon tape library one day and found a group session tape labeled 'Carmen Lago leaves Synanon.' It was common to tape group sessions at Synanon. On the tape, they told my mother, 'You know we understand that you want to leave with this guy Louie.' I heard my mother saying, 'I'm taking Nora.' Then my dad's screaming at the top of his lungs, 'You are not fucking touching her. You do what you got to do, but you're not going to touch her.' "

Nora's mother and Louie flew back to New York. "Neither side of the family would take them in because they couldn't believe that my mother left me. So my mom and Louie had nowhere to go. Everything she owned was in two suitcases. They lived in abandoned buildings and one day

Carmen Lago and her daughter, Nora Lago.

their luggage was stolen. All of my baby pictures were stolen, which broke my mother's heart. My mother got so down and out that she started using drugs again.

"Now, I'm glad my father did what he did because of the way she ended up after she left the program. He said that he was going to take care of me, and he did. I'm not a religious person but I thank God or whatever being it is for that. If I had gone with my mother, who knows where I would be. My dad did the right thing. I took that hate I felt for him and I turned it around in my own gut and said, 'He was looking out for what was best for me. And if he hadn't, I wouldn't have been adopted by Chuck and Betty Dederich.' "

When Nora was fourteen, her father also decided to leave the program. He wanted Nora to go with him but Nora wanted to stay. At the time she was living on a 3,500-acre ranch in northern California owned by the program. It had horses and cattle, and everybody she grew up with lived there. Nora's father allowed her to stay but only if she would visit him. Nora stayed, but the visits were infrequent and only happened for a year.

"About a week after my father left," Nora recalls, "the founder of the program, Chuck Dederich, and his wife, Betty, invited me to dinner. He was white and she was black. I was fourteen years old and so nervous. They sat me down to tell me, 'We've known you since you were three years old. You have no parents here, and we're going to adopt you. You have no future with your parents. Your future is here.'

"It was an honor to be adopted by them. I got the royal treatment after that. They tried to adopt me legally, but they needed my parents' consent. My parents said no! I did change my name to Dederich, but not legally. I got the red carpet treatment, because once a Dederich touched you, you were gold. I was going to school in a limousine and getting a lot of things that the other kids weren't getting. Chuck and Betty had so much money that I was taking flying lessons. We had our own fleet of planes. I had a motorcycle. We had transportation you would not believe.

"Betty really took a liking to me and even went as far as saying, 'Why don't you start calling Chuck and me Mom and Dad?' I had a hard time with that. I would try, but I didn't feel like they were my mom and dad. I still loved my real mother and father."

Although from the time she was fifteen until she was nineteen, Nora had no contact with her parents, occasionally she would get a letter that her mother had written her. Sometimes the letters would get to her months after they were written. "I would cry and just say, 'God, she still knows where I'm at.'

"Chuck and Betty sat me down and said, 'You should cut your parents off. You should write them a letter saying you don't need them anymore because we're taking care of you now.' So I did it. I wrote them a Dear John letter and said, 'I'd really appreciate it if both of you don't talk to me, don't call me, don't write me—nothing.' Not that I really wanted to, but I did what I was told to do. I found out later that that really broke my mom's heart."

Throughout this time, Betty played a large role in Nora's life. "When I turned eighteen, Betty put me into a sales program and I got to travel. Betty would throw parties and have me host them. She had me wear dresses. She sent me to an etiquette school and taught me how to eat properly, how to address people, how to write a formal letter. I went to all these places and started to realize that people out in the real world weren't as bad as they said at Synanon. I think Betty knew that place was not going to last forever, and wanted to help me out."

Betty also cared that Nora was educated. When Nora came home with bad grades one day, Betty sat her down and told her, "Nora, I know that we've adopted you, but if you want to be a Dederich, and be a part of this royal family, I'm not going to raise you as a dumb Puerto Rican." Nora says, "I was starting to get a little pissed off at this conversation." Betty continued, "Because I never wanted to be a dumb nigger. Do you read?" "No," Nora said. "Well, here are some books," she said. "You have a month to read them, and I want you to tell me everything about each book." Nora says, "I became a bookworm after that and my grades went up. Even though she was very, very strict, I think that Betty was one of the most wonderful people that ever touched me. She was just an angel. She set an example for me and she did it well. I was also very scared of her, because she was this high priestess."

When Nora was eighteen years old, Betty died of lung cancer. "I'd never seen anybody die before. I felt like I was being abandoned again. My mom left me, and now this woman was leaving me too. That was one of the reasons I left Synanon. I didn't have any reason to be there anymore."

Nora called her dad, who had been living in Southern California, and he arranged for her to join him. Within a week of leaving Synanon, Nora bought a ticket to New York and went to see her mother. "I loved my mom so much and even though I went through that whole feeling of hating her and disowning her, underneath, I loved her and I had to go see her. She always stayed in touch with my dad. So I got her number from him, called her up, and said I'm coming to see you. She said, 'Come right now! I would love to see you.'

"I didn't even know what she was going to look like, but of all the people in LaGuardia Airport, I picked her out. I saw her and we just hugged." Nora spent two weeks getting reacquainted with her mother, and discovered that much had changed.

"She put herself in a program called Project Return in Manhattan. Eventually she ran the entire program and became the director of the facility. She retired about three years ago after twenty-five years of service and she's doing great. A lot of my characteristics are from her, like my sense of humor. I'm also very real and I love real people and she's that way, very down to earth. I think I am very affectionate because of her. I also recognize that I have an addictive personality and

that's from not just my mom, but my dad too. When I saw myself get caught in drugs, I was able to say, 'Hey, this is not the right thing.' So I pulled myself out of it. Nobody told me what to do; I just did it.

"My mom and I became really close. I would call her and tell her the most secret things and it was really nice. She's the least judgmental person I know. I can literally tell her anything. I think she would have loved for me to come live with her when she left Synanon. I still wish that she had taken me with her, but I know she couldn't. I know that if she did, I wouldn't be where I'm at today. I do have some resentment because she raised my brother Anthony and did a damn good job. But she couldn't do that with me. She was in an organization that told her what to do. That's what I finally came to understand later on. It wasn't my mother's fault, so I don't hold that against her." ∎

Nora Lago and her mother, Carmen Lago. Nora holds a photograph of children from the Synanon Church.

The Chosen One

Christy Haubegger

AND HER MOTHER,

Ann Haubegger

Christy Haubegger is the visionary founder of *Latina*, the first bilingual magazine targeted exclusively to Hispanic women in the United States. *NBC Nightly News* with Tom Brokaw recently profiled the Houston, Texas, native as one of the most inspirational women of the year. She was also chosen by *Crain's New York Business* as one of the most successful young businesswomen in America and by the Ms. Foundation for Women as one of the Top 10 Role Models of the Year. ■ Ann Haubegger is the remarkable woman who adopted Christy as an infant and raised her to have pride in her Mexican heritage.

WHEN CHRISTY HAUBEGGER was a little girl, she remembers a time when kids were standing around bragging that they knew where they came from. When they said they came from their mommy's tummy, Christy would smile and top their stories with something more dramatic. "Well, that's nice, but I was adopted!" she said. Christy thought that being adopted was the best way to come into the world. Her adoptive mother, Ann Haubegger, made sure that Christy knew she was special from the very beginning. She knew her daughter would need to arm herself against the battles to come.

"When I was five years old, I wrote a little story about myself. It said, 'My name is Christy. I'm five years old and I was adapted.' My teacher called my mom and said, 'Well, she's really bright and she is rather well adaptcd.' " Christy laughs at the memory and says, "I was very proud of that. Even now, when I tell people I'm adopted, they'll say, 'Oh, I'm so sorry.' But I think it's interesting because I have a pretty good idea of what my life would have been like if I hadn't been adopted and I think I did all right."

When Christy was born in Houston, Texas, her birth mother made an informal arrangement with her doctor to give up her child. The doctor knew that Ann, another one of his patients, was looking to adopt. The Haubeggers, a white couple, were ecstatic when they learned that Christy was up for adoption. The fact that the baby happened to be Mexican-American did not matter to Ann or her husband, who was adopted himself. Ann could not love her little girl any more if she came from her own body.

Shortly thereafter, the Haubeggers adopted a little boy who became Christy's brother. "My brother was adopted a year after me. The two of us are really close in age. My parents initially thought about adopting three or four kids, then they decided that we should not outnumber them."

Ann never tried to hide the fact of Christy's adoption from her. "They told me that I was special because I was chosen. And for a long time I believed this wonderful mythology that they picked me because I was the prettiest baby they'd ever seen. I sort of believed that until fairly recently."

One of the things that Christy remembers is how different she and her mom were from the very beginning. "It's funny for me to look at pictures of us," she says. "I see this baby with thick black hair and my mother is blonde and very different-looking. I think it would have been very weird for me to grow up in Indianapolis, in a whole blonde world.

But I grew up in Houston, in a town that's more than thirty percent Hispanic. I didn't grow up feeling like I was from Mars. I grew up with a very good sense of 'Oh, there are lots of people like me,' which is good."

And Ann made sure that Christy remained connected to her Latino roots. "It was really important for my mother that I learned to speak Spanish." Christy recalls, "She made me start learning Spanish when I was four. I'm not great, but I'm pretty comfortable speaking in Spanish. I remember I wanted to take French in high school because all the cool kids were taking French. My mother said, 'Absolutely not.' I think my mother didn't want me to be embarrassed when people came up to me asking questions in Spanish.

"My mother didn't want me to feel bad about who I was because, frankly, Texas in the seventies probably wasn't the greatest place to be Mexican-American. She didn't want me to feel like being Mexican-American was a bad thing even though the world often said it was. Knowing full well that the world wasn't always a kind place, I think in some ways my mother really overcompensated. She told me all the time that I was beautiful and capable and I could do anything I wanted to do, so I would have all this positive stuff stored up."

But curbing her daughter's stubborn streak took early discipline. "I must have been about three years old, and my mother told me to pick up the toys that I had spread around in the living room," Christy laughs as she recounts one of her mother's favorite

Christy Haubegger and her mother, Ann Haubegger.

stories. "I said, 'No. I'm not going to pick them up,' and she said, 'Fine. You're gonna sit here on this chair until you pick them up.' She had a chair set up in the middle of the room and I sat there for an hour, which is a really long time for a three-year-old. After a while, she said, 'Okay, that's it. You're getting a spanking and you're going up to your room.' And she spanked my little butt and sent me up the stairs to my room. About halfway up the stairs I turned around and said, 'That didn't hurt.' I think my mother took the stairs four at a time and I got the spanking of my life."

Christy has fond memories of growing up in Texas. She was raised in the house her grandparents built. Both she and her brother were extremely active and Ann gave her children a lot of freedom to explore their world. "My mother was this amazing person who could deal with any crisis." Christy explains, "My brother and I would fall out of things and break our bones. If we did something horrible like splitting our heads open, we couldn't go to Dad because he would nearly faint. But my mom could apply pressure to the wound while driving us to the hospital. She really was amazing that way.

"I thought my mother was the toughest person in the world. She was the leader of my Girl Scout troop and I even saw her kill a snake that was near our campsite. I saw my mother chop that snake to bits with a hoe. As a very small child I was thinking, 'You don't want to mess with that lady.' "

As the kids were growing up, Ann wanted to make sure that she passed down her tough work ethic to her children. Christy says her mother didn't grow up with as much as she and her brother did. "We weren't wealthy by any means; we were just middle-class people, but my mother was always worried that we'd grow up like spoiled kids. I think for her there's nothing worse than a spoiled child.

"My mother cleaned all the time and even now I think that my idea of a clean house and my mother's idea of a clean house are really far apart. She came to visit me recently and I had the woman who cleans my house clean it from top to bottom. My mother came in, looked around, and said, 'I realize you haven't had time to clean.' My mother did everything—she worked, cleaned the house, cooked us every meal, and took us everywhere we needed to go. She did everything and made it seem effortless. Now I think to myself, 'How did she do that?' "

Aside from being a superwoman housewife, Ann has been a successful headhunter for a personnel agency for over thirty years. "I work some crazy hours and it's all I can do to keep myself in clean clothes and to keep myself fed," Christy admits. "I'm embarrassed that I have someone clean my house. What excuse do I have when my mother worked full-time and raised two children and had a husband?"

Working in the area of medical personnel, Ann has established herself as top recruiter in one of the most demanding fields. "Her career really blossomed once my brother and I left the house" Christy says. "It's really great to see that now that my parents are in their sixties, they travel all the time. They're even going to Honduras. But when we were growing up, their idea of a vacation was to get in a car and drive to other parts of Texas. We never went to Disney World as children, but they've been to Disney World as adults."

Christy says that much of her

Christy Haubegger and her mother, Ann Haubegger, make tortilla soup.

success is due to her mother reinforcing her sense of pride and self-esteem in being a Latina. Because of this constant positive reinforcement about her culture and heritage, Christy has always been acutely aware when it was missing. "I started a magazine for Latinas because more than most people, I could see the absurdity of the fact that Latinas weren't in the media. I think everyone else sort of accepts it in some ways because if you don't see yourself in magazines, newspapers, or on television, you could at least go home and find people who look like you. Maybe I started the magazine because I didn't have that as an option."

Christy received a degree in philosophy from the University of Texas at Austin and went on to earn her juris doctorate from Stanford Law School, where she was president of her class. Her position as senior editor of the *Stanford Law Review* gave her a taste for publishing and journalism. So in one of her marketing courses, she created a business plan for a publication that would become *Latina* magazine. "A lot of people assume because my parents are white, they put this expectation of overachievement on me and that's not true. A couple of years ago I received a card from my dad and it said he just wanted me to know how proud he and my mother were of me, not because of what I've done but because of who I am. I think if you ask my parents, 'What is your definition of having raised a successful child?' they would say someone who is decent and generous and kind and fun to be around. Nowhere in the equation would there be educational attainment or income or being recognized by the media. Their idea of success would be that I'd be a decent, kind, and generous person."

Coming to terms with her Latina identity did not come without some soul-searching. "I used to feel like my experience as a Latina was in some way inauthentic—that I have a less Latina life because I was raised by white parents. I used to think, 'Who am I to be starting this magazine?' But the truth is that I had this unique perspective to do the magazine because of my own experience of being raised between two worlds—my mother's world and that of my Mexican heritage. Maybe in some ways I could see something that other people couldn't see. Maybe that vantage point gave me this opportunity.

"I still have this very romantic notion of the American dream. You can do anything. I think my mother believed that for me. I also think my birth mother believed that for me because by giving me up, she felt the best chance I would have would be elsewhere. And she's probably right in some ways."

While the fact that Ann and her daughter are of different races has had a definite impact, it has not defined their core mother-daughter relationship. "While my mother couldn't hand me my Latina identity, she surely handed me the tools to find my identity as a woman. She gave me the tools to find out who I am and reinforced positive values in me. I think that's really what parents should do—give their children tools to figure it out. Your biological parents determine certain genetic things about you but they don't really get to determine who you are—your character and your spirit. Great parents give you the opportunity to find all those things, which is what my mother did."

While these two women share much between them, Ann has always been clear that she sees Christy as a daughter more than a friend. There was a time in high school when it seemed like the mothers of all of Christy's friends wanted to be their daughters' best friends. Ann had to set her daughter straight. "My mom would tell me I don't need any more friends," Christy reports. " 'You have plenty of friends. You need a mother.' So I got a very clear sense of hierarchy."

A question that Christy had to confront was whether she would ever want to begin the search to find her birth mother. More than a simple inquiry, it is a complicated and emotional process that forces an adopted child to examine the reasons behind the need to know. "I've resolved the question about finding my birth mother a long time ago," Christy explains. "If I felt that this person could provide something

I'm missing, I would look for her. But, I would not want to force those expectations on someone. And truthfully, she hasn't come to find me either." Christy adds, "Sometimes 'family' is defined as the people you're related to and sometimes it's the people who love you. Hopefully they are one and the same, but that's not always the case. I think it's really hard, particularly for Latinas, because we have high expectations of what family should be and when they're not what we expect, we don't know what to do."

Ann has told Christy that she would support her search for her birth mother if that were what she wanted to do. And Christy admits there have been periods of time when she wanted to find her birth mother. "I think the times I wanted to find her was when I was a teenager and when I was going through an identity crisis. Everything is a question mark when you're a teenager. But thank God I didn't. I have three good friends who found

their birth mothers and they have had really disappointing experiences. They found people who didn't want to be found, people with all kinds of problems that you wouldn't think of. The truth is most people who put children up for adoption don't do it because their lives are so great. It's not something you do when you have other alternatives. Most women who put their children up for adoption come to the point where they realize they're just not going to be able to make it work. And that situation probably hasn't changed. Sure, I would like to have some health history. There are practical matters like that, but I don't think finding my birth mother is gonna help me understand more about my life or myself.

"Weirdly enough, I get told I look like people all the time, so I start thinking, 'My God.' One time, my dad approached some woman in a bank that he thought was me. He walked up to the woman and said, 'What are you doing here?' I always wonder, 'Do I have thousands of cousins running around or am I just the standard stock-issue Latina, short and curvy?'

"People talk about nature versus nurture, and I believe in nature. I believe a lot of things in my character are probably from my birth mother. But what I did with those things was completely my experience, my environment and me. I have a tendency to be really, really stubborn but I have a choice about what to do with my stubbornness. I could be a jerk or I could become a really determined person who achieves what she sets out to do. You can take that same little trait, but you can turn it in two different directions. I can also choose to look at my adoption in two different ways—I can say I was rejected or I can say I was deeply loved. To tell you the truth, I would rather think I was deeply loved. And I have my mother to thank for that.

"I just hope to make my mother feel like adopting me was something that she never regrets. It must have been scary to have a baby she knew nothing about and just decide to love me for a long time before I was lovable. I admire her so much for that." ■

An Independent Woman

Cristina Saralegui

AND HER MOTHER,

Cristy S. Saralegui

Cristina Saralegui is the force behind and the center of a media empire that includes her Emmy Award–winning television show, *The Cristina Show*, on Univision, watched weekly by over one hundred million viewers, *Cristina* magazine, and a radio program, *Cristina Opina*. In addition, Cristina established Arriba la Vida/Up With Life Foundation, which is dedicated to AIDS awareness in the Latin community. ■ While she and her mother may be from different worlds, Cristina credits her mother with giving her one of her most valuable gifts: the ability to be an independent woman.

AN INDEPENDENT WOMAN

FOR CRISTINA SARALEGUI, Cuba during the fifties was a time of elegance and excitement. She was born in Miramar, a drowsy, idyllic, and very wealthy suburb of Havana, "where everyone's main worry was that during the hurricane season, his or her yacht was secured at the country club they belonged to." Because her grandfather was a millionaire who co-owned the most important Spanish-language magazines on the island, *Bohemia, Carteles,* and *Vanidades,* Cristina grew up meeting movie stars, singers, and literary giants such as Ernest Hemingway within her grandfather's wood-paneled offices. And, in the midst of the entire spectacle, Cristina's mother, Cristy Saralegui, stood out.

"I remember my mother was very fashionable in those years," Cristina recalls. "She was a woman with lots of style who always looked spectacular. She had a collection of rings she wore on her little finger and she wore her collar up. That wasn't done back then. She never followed the fashion trends of her time, and she taught me how to be elegant in my own way, to set my own style. That's why I have my own style, my own look. I don't have to worry about reading forty fashion magazines to figure out what to wear because I know what looks good on me and what doesn't. My mother taught me to define my own style as a woman."

Fortunately for Cristina, her mother's style had as much to do with action as appearance. "My mother taught me not to shut my mouth and always say what I think," she explains. "That's because my father never told my mother 'shut up' at the dinner table. She was always a total equal partner with my father—in business, in bed, everywhere. She taught me that in relationships I could not settle for any less."

Cristy was born to working-class parents in Pinar Del Rio, Cuba, a city where tobacco was grown. "When my mother and father fell in love," Cristina says, "it became a problem because she was from a different social class and his family said she was a peasant." Cristina's father's family objected to the marriage of their son and his girlfriend not only because of their class differences but because she was a woman too unusual for her times. "When my mother was young," Cristina explains, "Cuban women did not work or drive automobiles. But she had a little Fiat Topolino, which looked like an egg and which she drove from the time she was sixteen." Cristy also had a job as a hostess with Pan American, greeting the VIPs who traveled to Cuba on that airline. "She even went as far as rebelling against the conventions that ruled Cuban girls' lives, and decided to go to Miami with my father and a group of friends, without a chaperone! My father decided to marry her anyway. He just sent them an invitation, and that was that." Once the family got over the shock, they were left with no choice but to give the pair a grand wedding in a church in Miramar.

"My mother was always treated as one of the boys," says Cristina. "So I was brought up to be one of the boys and I am one of the boys. When the men used to go fishing, my mom would be the only woman they would take with them. And she would fish better than they would. My mother was proud of the fact that she would not only go fishing with the men, but that she would pee out in the woods like them as well." Unlike many of her contemporaries, Cristy knew how to balance being assertive with being feminine. "When the men played poker, the one that would beat them all was my mom. She was also one of the boys when it came to rights, when it came to money, and when it came to ambitions. But at the same time, I learned from my mom that I had to be feminine and stylish. She taught me to use my brain as power."

In 1960, the world turned upside down for the Saralegui family. Fidel Castro's guerrilla army toppled the existing government and Castro's forces made a victorious entry into Havana. Soon, the new Cuban government became friendly with the USSR, seized nearly all U.S.-owned properties in Cuba, and made further agreements with other Communist governments. As a result of Castro's Communist revolution, thousands of Cubans fled the country, including the Saralegui family.

Without warning his children, Cristina's father devised a plan to get his wife and children safely off the island without the authorities suspecting. They did not tell the eleven-year-old Cristina that they were leaving until the night before they actually left Cuba. "I went out and put my hands out to the breeze, that beautiful tropical breeze of my island, and I looked out at the sea and saw the moon falling over it. They didn't let me call my friends. I couldn't say good-bye to anyone because our phones were tapped. I remember that I looked at the view and, you know when you are drinking a really good drink and you drink it slowly so that you can enjoy it? Well, I took in that view and I drank and drank and drank because I knew that I would never see it again."

The last image that Cristina has of Cuba was the Havana airport waiting room, where her father dropped his family before they left the island. "Part of my parents' elaborate plan to leave the island was to have mother take the four children on 'vacation' to Trinidad first, then wait for my father to join us. I remember my father standing at the airport with tears in his eyes because he didn't know if he was ever going to be able to leave the island. We thought that we would never see each other again. We were leaving everything that meant anything to us. We knew we shouldn't cry, because if we did, then the authorities would know what was going on."

As Cristina's mother left for an uncertain future in Trinidad, she realized that for the first time in her life, she was truly on her own. "My dad wrote my mother often during those eight months," Cristina says. "My mom also wrote him and wrote him. One day I broke a drawer and I read the letters. You can't imagine the desperate letters that man wrote to that woman. So I know what they did on their honeymoon!"

Once in exile, the Saralegui family had to adapt to a new reality. "Because my father spoiled my mother, she didn't know how to cook. She had never been a housewife and, in fact, she didn't know how to clean or do anything around the house—and neither do I. We used to say she was trying to poison us because whenever she tried to cook she burned everything and salted everything too much. But she had to learn out of necessity. I can say she is a pretty good cook now."

Eight months after being separated from his wife, Cristina's father was able to join his family in Key Biscayne, Florida. "Key Biscayne wasn't what it is today," Cristina recalls. "It was a small barrio. It wasn't a millionaire's town; it was a project town. Every time it rained or there were hurricanes, the streets would flood. You could catch fish out on the streets with your bare hands." Despite the fact that their new life in the United States was drastically different than

Cristina Saralegui and her mother,
Cristy S. Saralegui.

what they had known in Cuba, Cristina was simply happy to have her family reunited.

Although Cristy knew that their exile was a permanent one, she never let their children know. "What I remember most from those times is how much fun we used to have. Ever since we came to America, my parents did everything possible for us to believe that we were on vacation. Our parents never gave us the anxiety that comes with being in exile. They would say, 'We're going to stay here for a year. We're going to go to a new school. We're going to speak English.' They made a great effort to make sure we fit in."

Although little by little Cristina adapted to life in America, Cristy made certain that her daughter did not totally lose the Cuban values that they were raised with. That is why Cristina was chaperoned to all of her school parties until she was eighteen years old. "My mom came to get us from one party and she saw all those American kids kissing each other and there were no parents there. She told me, 'This is the last school party that you're coming to.' And from then on she sent her father, Abuelo Pelusa, out with me."

Another family member recruited to escort the young Cristina to those wild American teen parties was her aunt Tita. "My aunt Tita used to come with me to the Immaculate Conception dances and when I went to dance with a boy, she used to walk up to us with her purse and white sweater and tell us, 'Separate yourselves, or I'm going to have to tell your father. And if you continue this behavior, I'm not going to chaperone you anymore.' There was a point when being my chaperone became such a big job that we couldn't find anyone to do it anymore. Mom told us, 'You can't go out without a chaperone. I'm not going to do it, so you better find someone else.' " As chaperones became more and more difficult to line up, Cristina finally decided that she had had enough. Following in the true spirit of her mother, one day Cristina marched up to her mother and told her she was going out with her boyfriend without a chaperone. "And from that day on, I never had a chaperone. And that was that."

Although the Saralegui family had been well-to-do in Cuba, they were suddenly faced with the hard economic realities of living as exiles. Cristina's father pulled her out of college just nine credits short of graduating. "He pulled me out because he needed the money to pay for my brother's school, which used to be very expensive. At that time I was very glad that he pulled me out because I never really needed school. My brother needed his degree, because without his engineering degree, he wouldn't have been anything in life. God moves his pieces however he wants."

So Cristina began working for *Vanidades*, the magazine her family had founded and had just sold to a Venezuelan publisher. After working and becoming quite successful within the publishing world, Cristina stunned her parents by announcing that she was leaving to work in television. "My mother said, 'Are you crazy? Do you know how much money you make? Do you know how well you are doing? Are you going to risk all of this? You are not well.' She told me not to do it. And I thought, '*Coño*, this is the woman that has pushed me all my life. She's been the wind beneath my sails.' " Once again, Cristina found herself taking a stand and following her heart against the objections of her mother.

But Cristina had discovered that following her heart was the most rewarding thing she could do, both in terms of her business decisions and in her personal relationships. It was the very thing that her mother had done all her life.

"When I met my husband, Marcos, I was a very cynical professional woman who didn't believe in love. Then something funny happened: I fell in love. And it was the first time in my life that I was in love and I was very lucky to find my husband. I was meant for him, he was meant for me. We found each other and our lives changed completely. He told me, 'You have to leave the magazine, you have to move on to television.' He saw something in me that not even my parents had seen, especially my mother. So my parents felt threatened because Marcos saw so many things in me, and he still does. They said, 'Don't do this, don't get married,' which was the worst advice my mother had ever given me."

Marcos and Cristina married and, like her parents, they decided that they would be equal partners. "When Marcos came to my life, he asked, 'What do you want for you?' I said, 'I want this and this and this,' and Marcos had the intellectual power to make me succeed. Can you imagine? He was a twenty-four-year-old boy and I was a thirty-five-year-old

woman. And yet he taught me to understand myself."

Cristina credits her husband for teaching her to be more affectionate. "I am physically affectionate with my kids because my husband taught me how. He grew up with three women, all Cuban, and they all hugged the hell out of him. But my mother never hugged me because my mother's mother never hugged her. I was sure she loved me and I am sure she loves me now, but it wasn't physical.

"When I left home for the first time, my mother would call me and tell me all these things and I would just sit there and listen. It was very hard at the beginning because my mom was very bossy. Bossy and rotten. Then one day Marcos came in and said, 'Why don't you just hang up on her?' I thought, '*Coño*, I have the option to hang up.' I said, 'Bye, Mami,' and I hung up. That's when she realized that she could no longer change our relationship. I had to hang up on her lots of times.

"I learned to dominate my mother in order to liberate myself. I said, 'Good-bye, Mom, see you later,' and bang, I disconnected her because there was nothing she could do

Cristina Saralegui and her mother,
Cristy S. Saralegui.

anymore. It's psychological. Little by little I started to cut out that dependency that I didn't like. It is very difficult when you grow up with a very strong mother, establishing your own personality when ninety percent of the things you believe in, she doesn't. Then you grow up and they don't like that."

In raising her own children, Cristina is proud to say that she learned to take all the good things about her mother and not repeat the things that she considered bad. "I really don't care to intervene in my children's lives in the same way my mother intervened in mine. I don't call them all the time nor do I tell them what to do. I make suggestions. I talk to them. They come to my bed and they ask me, 'What do you think I should do with this?' I have a very intense life so I don't need to live through my children. The relationship I have with my children is very different than the relationship I had with my parents after I became independent and could decide what I wanted for myself. My parents came from another world, from another time."

One of the most important lessons Cristina did learn from her mother is to have everyone else respect her. "That's something she did since she was a little girl," Cristina explains. "Her parents respected her, her husband respected her, but that's the way she is. She is a strong woman."

It was this ability to demand respect that has served Cristina so well in business. "It was very difficult to be accepted by the men in my business, especially from Latino men. Sometimes I would ask my father things about the magazine business and no matter what I asked or said, he would always tell me that he had done it bigger or better. All the advice he would give me would only work in his time. He was from another world. What I can do is listen to my parents and tell them what I think, but I can't give them advice because I am from another world. The difference between my parents and me is that I know that."

While in many ways, Cristina would not want to live in her mother's world, there remains, however, much that Cristina admires about her mom and her world. "My mom was my inspiration to understand that a woman had to reach her aspirations. I never told my mom how much I admired her style when I used to sit there and watch her get dressed. I never told her how I dreamed about going fishing with the men the way she did. I never said thank you for making me a person that uses her brain and not her body to get what she wants. She taught me to be independent and what it means to be a real woman, which has nothing to do with appearance, it is all in the inside. It has to do with the feminine energy to procreate and creativity to do whatever you want to do. That is what my mother taught me." ∎

Unanswered Questions

Aida Rodriguez

AND HER MOTHER,

Ana Lucia Rodriguez

Aida Rodriguez has always been interested in law enforcement. After serving as a street cop for a number of years, she is now in charge of community outreach for the Metropolitan Police Department in Washington, D.C. She works as a liaison between the police department and the community. ■ Although Ana Lucia Rodriguez is not Aida's biological mother, she is certainly her mother in spirit. Ana runs her own cleaning business, where she's in charge of several women. But the most important work she has done is in accepting a young girl she didn't know as her own daughter.

WHEN AIDA RODRIGUEZ left Nicaragua, she was five years old and terrified. Her mother put her on the plane headed for Maryland to live with a man she didn't know: her father. "I remember that trip. I remember I was wearing a short, little dress and I hardly had any hair. And I remember that I didn't want to leave. My mother put my brother and me on the plane by ourselves all the way from Nicaragua. My brother was four years old and we fought the whole time because we both wanted the window seat."

Although she spent her early years in Nicaragua, Aida was actually born in Hyattsville, Maryland. It was there that her father met her biological mother, Mariana. After the couple discovered that Mariana was pregnant, they married and had Aida and her brother shortly thereafter. When the marriage fell apart, Mariana took her two children with her to Nicaragua, where her mother and family lived. Aida's memories of her mother in Nicaragua are blurry at best. "All I remember is my grandmother in Nicaragua because my mother was hardly ever there. We stayed in Nicaragua until she decided to ship us back to my father in Maryland."

While she didn't realized it at the time of that memorable airplane flight, Aida's parents had been waging a fierce battle over her and her brother. Aida says, "My father wanted us back. When I got older, my father told me all this stuff that he used to do, like send us money. He said he wanted to see us but that she would never let us talk to him. I guess when he stopped sending us money is when she wanted to get rid of us and that's when we came here. At least that's the story that I got.

"When we arrived at the airport my dad and stepmom were waiting for us there. I did not recognize my father. I was very scared."

Waiting for the little girl at the airport was Ana Lucia Rodriguez, the new wife of Aida's father. Born and raised in Costa Rica, Ana was just as anxious to meet the children she had heard so much about. "When I first got here Ana received me with open arms," Aida recalls. "But it was sort of weird because she was not my mother. So I guess she didn't really know how to act."

As difficult as it was to come to a new country as a child, to make that trip without her mother and to meet a father she didn't remember was nothing short of terrifying for Aida. "Because my brother and I only spoke Spanish, we had to learn to speak English. I had to start school and go to English as a second language classes."

Aida's stepmother, Ana, had a daughter from a previous marriage who also lived in the house. Although Aida was initially wary of the older girl, she turned out to be a valuable big sister to her and her brother by helping them through this period of adjustment. And Ana turned out to be more of a mother than a stepmother.

"My stepmom treated us like a real mom from the beginning," Aida explains. "She treated us just like she did her own daughter. Later my father and Ana had a daughter together, so I then had a younger sister. When Ana cooked a meal she fed us all the same thing. She always treated us equally as if we were her real children. In fact, sometimes I think she gave us special attention because she wanted to find a way to make us feel comfortable."

As hard as Ana tried, it took a while for her stepdaughter to feel at home. When children would make fun of her Nicaraguan accent or her shyness, it was Ana that she would run to. "I would come home saying, '*Los chabales no quieren jugar conmigo*,' " Aida recalls. "I would come home and start crying because they didn't want to play with me."

As Aida slowly grew to accept her new mother and her new world, she continued to hold on to the hope that her biological mother would someday return for her. Aida says, "I always used to think she would come. But when I was in Nicaragua, I remember that I was with my grandmother and my older brothers more than I was with my mother. I guess it wasn't that I thought my mom would come back, but I always thought I was going to go back home to Nicaragua to see the rest of the family."

Aida has some information about her mother but Mariana remains a mystery. Although her biological mother and her family live in Nicaragua, she told her daughter that she was Dominican. Later, Aida uncovered Mariana's birth certificate, which said she was born in Puerto Rico. She also discovered that her mother had four other children that Aida never knew existed.

Ana Rodriguez and her stepdaughter, Aida Rodriguez, in Washington, D.C.

The children of divorce and adoption often have more questions than answers. Aida is not interested in judging her mother for sending her away, but she would like to know why. "I don't think she did it for economic reasons in my case," Aida speculates. "My dad showed me the money orders that he used to send to my mom in Nicaragua when we were there. I mean she had a maid and her mom lived there. And she still gave us away. I found out that she remarried and my dad didn't know. When she went out to Nicaragua she remarried and had another child. There were a lot of lies there. I hurt for my dad.

"It hurts because I don't understand how my mother could just leave me like that. And what made it worse was that my relationship with my father was not always great. It just made it worse."

Surprisingly, Aida found the most comfort and support in

her relationship with Ana. While the two women don't share flesh and blood, Ana is the woman Aida now refers to as mother. She explains, "Mariana is my biological mother but Ana is my mother. She's my mother. When I talk about Mariana, I call her my biological mother and Ana is my mother.

"Ana has always been there for me. I could go to her before I could go to my dad about anything. I guess I'm a little scared of my dad. But my mom was the one I went to if I had any problems, like when I started my period."

Aida would also join her stepmother on her job cleaning houses. Ana now runs her own cleaning service in the Washington, D.C., area. "Ever since I could remember I would work with her," Aida says. "I would go out to work with her when we didn't have school. I would be with her so we could always talk."

Despite their great relationship, Ana and Aida faced problems like all mothers and daughters do. One such problem was when Aida discovered that she was pregnant her senior year of high school. "I almost dropped out of school, but I went back and graduated with my class. I graduated June sixth and I had my son June twenty-seventh."

Aida found herself facing the most difficult period in her life. She was eighteen years old with an infant son and moving from place to place when she decided to join the police academy as a cadet. "Ana was the only one helping me throughout this time because my dad didn't want to speak to me," Aida says. "She was always there. She helped me whenever I needed it. I was moving around a lot so I had to resign from the academy. Once I got my first apartment I started going to Montgomery College."

In college, Aida majored in criminal justice while trying to get back into the police department. During these busy times, Aida attended school while Ana watched her son. "Then my dad and I finally started talking again and they both started helping me," Aida says. "Ana helped me get my first car. Then I was hired again by the police department. She didn't want me to be a police officer because she was scared. But she said she would support me because this is what I've always wanted to do."

Aida now has a second son and she loves to hear her children call Ana "Grandma." Aida says, "My kids are her grandkids. I've told my son David a little bit about my life, *yo le hablo*, because he understands me. I told him how much Ana has done for me and he loves my mom. Every time he goes to her house, he asks for *platanos* and she cooks everything he says he wants to eat. I work two jobs and my parents take care of my sons for me. They are always there."

Although Aida is in a great place in her life, on occasion she finds herself encountering her past and has to face the old unanswered questions again. A number of years ago, she saw her biological mother, Mariana. Aida heard that Mariana was in town and she realized she couldn't let the opportunity to talk to her slip past her. "She has another son from a previous relationship who was graduating from a local high school. So I went to see her. I just wanted to ask her, 'Why? How could you do this?' Not that I hated her, but I just want to know why, how could she just leave us?

"I got to see her and she gave me a hug and it just felt cold. She had nothing to say and that hurt. I was afraid to confront her because of what she might have said, so I didn't ask her anything."

Although she wasn't able to establish a connection with her biological mother, she did connect with a sister—one of Mariana's daughters.

Aida says, "I keep in contact by e-mail with one of her daughters, which is my sister, I guess. In the last couple of years, I also started e-mailing her two older sons. It's kind of hard because I have to write in Spanish. I still speak Spanish and I can read it, but writing it is difficult. I can't write to them as clearly as I'd like, so the communication is a little hard and they can't answer the questions that I have for them.

"Now that I'm a mother, I know I could never do to my boys what my mother did to me. I couldn't see giving them up and knowing what they would miss. My mother missed seeing me and my brother grow up and now she's missing her grandchildren growing up."

Even with all the unresolved questions, Aida has found a resolution in knowing that she has Ana to depend on. With a smile, Aida remembers the enormous act of kindness that greeted her as she first stepped off that plane from Nicaragua. "I thank her for taking care of me and my brother and accepting us like her kids." ■

The Storytellers

Nina Tassler

AND HER MOTHER,

Norma Grau Tassler

Nina Tassler has always been involved in the storytelling process, having begun her career at the Roundabout Theatre Company in New York City. Currently, Nina is the senior vice president of drama series development at CBS Entertainment. Nina oversees development of all of the network's primetime drama series, including *Judging Amy* and *CSI: Crime Scene Investigation.* ■ Nina's mother, Norma Grau Tassler, is a strong woman who, as a young immigrant to this country, took on the responsibility of helping to raise and support her family. Of the many invaluable things that Norma gave to her daughter, one of the most valuable has been the gift of telling stories.

THE STORYTELLERS

WHILE MANY WOMEN pass down antique jewelry or dusty heirlooms to their daughters, the women in the Grau family pass down something far more valuable—they pass down stories and a love of storytelling.

Nina remembers one story in particular. "My mother was at my grandmother's bedside and just before she died, she told my mother in typical Grau fashion, 'You're my only true daughter.' " The significance of her deathbed confession was that it had long been a part of Grau family lore that Nina's aunt Millie wasn't actually her grandmother's daughter. "My grandmother raised my aunt Millie, but there was all this speculation as to whether or not she was one of my grandmother's children or if she was born to my grandmother's sister. As my aunt got older in life, every family member used to speculate about whom she actually looked like.

"So for years I'm thinking my grandmother adopted my aunt Millie. When my aunt Millie passed away roughly three years ago, I said to my mother, 'How heartbreaking that must have been for her to never have known the truth about her identity or never to have been able to know that her aunt was her mother.' And my mother turned to me and said, 'What are you talking about?' I repeated the story about her aunt having aunt Millie out of wedlock and then having her adopted by her married sister. My mother looked at me with a perfectly straight face and said, 'Oh, I made that up.' " Nina laughs at the memory. "I lived my entire life believing that story!"

In a sense, for Latinas the telling of stories is more important than the story itself. More important than the details or the facts is the tradition of how these stories are passed down. As in the ancient tradition of oral histories, more than passing down a family's history, it is an opportunity for women to bond.

Nina says, "When I hear stories passed down in my family, you're not quite sure how much is truth and how much has been embellished over the years. But the truth is, like any good story, the story of my aunt haunted me. I fantasized about it and it has stayed with me because it's like a telenovela: there's families and premarital sex and children born out of wedlock. It really has given me permission in this crazy fantasy life to think anything is possible."

And for Nina, everything has proved to be possible. As senior vp of development at CBS, Nina has had the opportunity to bring life to many "crazy fantasies." Nina says, "When I first came to the network three years ago, *Judging Amy* was the first show that I really felt had my outlook on life and my relationship with my mother. The people who watch *Judging Amy* connect with the fact that the mother and daughter share a very special bond and have a kind of secret language and a way of communicating that sometimes nobody else can understand. There are times when my mother and I will say non sequitur, nonlinear things in the course of storytelling that only a mother and daughter would understand. *Judging Amy* was the first time that I felt that a television relationship was very well informed by my own relationship with my mother. Because I know it came from Amy Brenneman's life and her relationship with her mother, the show is very complicated and has many layers to it. When we were developing it, we were able to project on the television relationship what we learned with our real relationships with our mothers.

"That nonlinear, non sequitur quality of storytelling is a part of the culture I grew up with. It's a part of the way I look at the world. I think it may be special to Latin women."

Nina was raised in a family of strong Latin women who were proud of their culture. Nina's grandmother was born in Spain and then came to Puerto Rico, where she met and married Nina's grandfather. "There is an interesting combination of Latin influences in my family: Spanish and Puerto Rican. The intermarriages that took place in my family are like the United Nations. We have Mexican, Cuban, and South American. Every sort of Latin American country is represented in my family, just about."

Nina's mother, Norma, was the eldest in a large family. By the time she arrived in the United States, she was already the unofficial head of the household. She took care of her younger siblings and earned money

Norma Grau Tassler and her daughter, Nina Tassler.

by making clothing in the infamous New York sweatshops.

Norma told her daughter a story that her Spanish ancestors were Jewish and converted to Christianity during the Inquisition. "Those stories played a major part, a significant role in who we are and where we come from," Nina says. "The stories gave me a tremendous sense of pride, as I've always been raised Jewish." When Norma married Nina's father, she took the opportunity to convert to Judaism.

Nina says, "I was born in Washington Heights and all my family lived in the same building. My grandfather and my grandmother had a place off of the park. You had the *carniceria* right next to the Jewish butcher." When her grandparents moved to upstate New York, Nina's family moved with them.

"We were in upstate New York and we had many family members who lived within two miles of each other. I grew up with all of my aunts, uncles, and cousins. There was a connection to every family member. I have tremendous emotions in my heart and, to this day, I have a very intense connection to my family, my husband's family, and to my children. I pay attention to and respect those relationships.

Norma Grau Tassler and her daughter,
Nina Tassler.

"I have two children: a fourteen-year-old boy who is named for my father and a three-year-old girl who is named for my husband's grandmother and my grandmother, Risa. As we all become much more assimilated, somehow I keep trying to remind my children who we are with these stories. My son did a family tree for a class project, so he interviewed my mother and he got many stories from her about her experiences. And he listened to the stories of my grandparents, so he got some sense of the tradition. He knows the story of where we came from, of who his great-grandparents were, and the stories of my mother growing up.

"The older we get, we search for some kind of contact with our past and where we come from. My grandmother and my grandfather passed it on to my mother, who raised me with the stories."

Because Norma now lives in Florida and Nina and her family live in California, they don't spend as much time together as Nina would like. But this in no way diminishes the intense relationship that Nina witnesses between her mother and her three-year-old daughter.

"My mother is an unbelievable cook and whenever she gets together with my daughter, they're in the kitchen. They're always cooking, baking cookies, or making donuts. And they both love to sing. When I'm driving back and forth to work, I play a CD in the car and I give my daughter the cell phone so she can sing to Grandma in Florida at the top of her lungs. Thank God there's technology, it gives them a chance to sing to each other. It's the act of doing something together and passing that on to your granddaughter that's important."

More than fairy tales and myths, it is these stories of family, love, and connection that matter. Nina says, "The things my mother most clearly passed down to me were the emphasis on family and the need for storytelling." Ultimately, the stories that Norma gave to Nina are important because they are their shared history and the stories of their lives. ■

Soul Sisters

Rosario Dawson

AND HER MOTHER,

Isabel Dawson

At fifteen years old with no acting experience, Rosario Dawson was cast in her first feature film, Larry Clark's controversial *Kids*. After that, the young woman of Puerto Rican, Cuban, Irish, and Native American heritage has appeared in over fifteen Hollywood feature and independent films, including *Josie and the Pussycats*, *Men in Black 2*, and Spike Lee's *The 25th Hour*. ■ Rosario's mother, Isabel Dawson, forged the way for her actress daughter by demonstrating that the only expectations she had to live up to were her own. Mother and daughter have proved to themselves and to each other that there is little that they need beyond each other.

WHEN ROSARIO DAWSON was a little girl she always had to know where her mother was. "I would be in the other room playing," says Rosario, recalling the trick her mother played on her. "My mother would be in the kitchen on the other side of the apartment. All of a sudden, I'd go, 'Mami?' because I had to check up on her. I would start walking real slow to where I thought she was. If I couldn't find her by the time I got to the other end of the apartment, I'd scream, 'Mami!' desperate to see her. I was looking to see where I'd lost her. Then she'd appear and say, 'What?' She would always hide from me on purpose. But when my little brother would hide from her in the park, she would get all frantic. He would hide behind a tree and just watch her. I told her she got exactly what she deserved; she tortured me and now he tortured her."

It's not unusual that Rosario would always want to know where her mother was—Isabel Dawson has always had a close relationship with her daughter, at times more like siblings than mother and daughter. "I think we're just lighthearted people, so it naturally makes for a very comfortable relationship. The mother-daughter dynamic is always there, but she's not always the mother and I'm not always the daughter. Every once in a while it reverses. I think we figured each other out, which makes our relationship a lot of fun.

"When I was very little, before my brother was born, we would go to Manhattan Beach and hang out and watch my dad play basketball. We would just spend time with each other. She's very cool. She would give me something after she read

it and we'd sit and read together, not talking. We always spent time together."

Unlike the home she created for herself and her daughter, Isabel was raised with more traditional expectations of what a Latina should do and be. The child of a Cuban father and a Puerto Rican mother, Isabel grew up in the very urban worlds of Brooklyn and the Bronx. "My mom was raised the exact opposite of how she raised me," Rosario says. "When my mom grew up, she had to cook and clean and look after her brothers. She had a lot of responsibilities at an early age. She had to come home right after school and she wasn't trusted. She wanted to break out of that and one of the ways she could do that was by getting pregnant.

"She was sixteen when she got pregnant with me. She wasn't given knowledge about a lot of things. My mom had to discover a lot of things by herself because she couldn't get advice from her mother. It's not that her mother was being mean; it's just the way it was. If you were stupid, you would have to suffer the consequences."

Rosario and her mother have talked about the impact her birth has had on her mother's life and ambitions. "I know there's a lot of things that my mom would have wanted to do," Rosario says, "but I don't think that means that she regrets having me. I know she doesn't because we talked about it. But as a human being on this planet, you have ideas and dreams for yourself and then life hits you and you adjust to it. Sometimes you are still able to incorporate those desires and sometimes you continue down a different road. My mom is still very young; she's forty years old. She could do anything she wants, but the timing is different. She has just had to adjust."

Isabel has not only adjusted; she has made certain that her daughter didn't repeat the same mistakes she made. "My mother didn't want that same thing for me," Rosario says. "She wanted me to have a choice. If she told me to do some-thing and I did something else, she always let me know that I still had her support. I was never harassed or told 'I told you so' because I went against her advice. She told me, 'I made a lot of choices in my life and I had to deal with the consequences. I can give you information about those things and save you some time if you want to ask me about it. If you don't ask me and you do the exact opposite of what I say, you will still have to learn the same lesson that way. It's your life, but I love you and I'm here for you.' "

Isabel Dawson and her daughter,
Rosario Dawson.

And Isabel has always been true to her word, raising Rosario as a single parent in the same apartment building as Rosario's dad. "Yeah, they lived in the same building," Rosario explains. "I spent most of my time with my mom, but I lived with both of them pretty equally.

"I was Daddy's little girl until I was about five years old. Until then, I was very much like my dad and I wanted to be like him and dress like him. After that, my personality became like my mother's. After that, my mom and I were always together. We were inseparable. I think there's this thing between the two of us where we are like one person."

The same unquenchable spirit in Isabel has been passed on like a torch to her daughter. "I've learned a lot about being myself from being around her, like I can be very loud and be very affectionate and sociable—things that my dad isn't. My mom is more outgoing and gregarious than my dad. All of the drama, all of the hanging out, all of the ideas, the parties and having lots of friends, being outspoken, strong and personable— I got all of that from my mom, from being around her. I wasn't her shadow; I was like her sock or something. I was on her; I was a part of her. I was always by her side when I was little. The cool part is that she always treated me like I was an adult."

Rosario remembers trying to keep up with her mother as they walked through the streets of New York City. To Isabel, it was her daughter's responsibility to keep up with her. Rosario remembers with a smile the fact that her mother never slowed down to wait for her. "I'd be walking slower than she was because I was five feet shorter than she was. She'd be

Isabel Dawson and her daughter, Rosario Dawson.

holding my hand and I remember running next to her and in some ways I felt like I was a little person who she respected. I will always remember that."

In what is now a well-known and often-told story, Rosario's introduction to the world of film came about when she was sitting on the stoop of her mother's East Village apartment building in 1995. Filmmaker Larry Clark happened to see the fifteen-year-old Rosario and cast her in his low-budget film *Kids*, a brutal story of teenagers, sex, and drug abuse.

Recalling how she was "discovered," Rosario laughs. "Yeah, it was weird. I was just hanging out and it just happened. It was cool with my mom. She told me that ever since I was little I had gotten offers to do modeling or commercials because I was a very precocious child. I was always very confident and very happy, I smiled a lot and I got along with people very well. My dad said that when I was a little over a year old and we were getting baby pictures taken, I sort of just started posing for the photographer. The guy was like, 'Oh my God. I'm going to watch out for this one.'

"When I was cast in *Kids*, my parents were very cool about it. At that age they thought that I was old enough. I had gotten offers before, but they didn't think I was old enough and they would always say no. They didn't want to expose me to that stuff, but as I got older I could really look at the material myself and see if it's what I wanted to do. And it just happened that I wanted to do the film."

Granting her daughter the authority to make her own decisions may appear unusual for the typical Latina mother, but Isabel is hardly the typical mother. Recently, Isabel did something that was downright untypical for a mother celebrating her fortieth birthday: she had her hair cut into a Mohawk and had her tongue pierced.

Rosario explains that she was not at all surprised. "I definitely expect my mom to do things like that. She's a very impulsive person. She's wanted to get a Mohawk since she was very young. But her mother told her she couldn't do it until she was forty. My grandmother told her, 'If you really want to do it and if it's really that important, then you will still want to do it even twenty years from now. If you want to do it after you've thought about it for a long time, then you can have it done.' So she did it when she was forty. And you know, her hair is going to grow back."

It's very telling that Isabel had the independent spirit to shave her head but still honored her own mother by waiting until she was forty. Isabel is a bridge between a generation of Latinas who grew up under a strict and traditional upbringing to a generation who feel the freedom to do what they want. Rosario recalls the moment her grandmother saw her mother's brand-new haircut. "My grandmother was very shocked, but she was like, 'I don't want to say anything negative because with this haircut we are able to see your face more and you are beautiful.' My grandmother thought she looked beautiful because she does."

The most beautiful thing about Isabel and Rosario, however, is how they love each other. Rosario says that some of her fondest childhood memories are the times she was able to curl up in Isabel's lap, with her arms wrapped around her protectively. She says, "I feel kind of sad about the fact that she can't curl me up like she used to, but she still does every once in a while. My mom grabs me and holds me in her lap, except now her legs start to give." ∎

Never Standing Still

Sandra Garcia

AND HER MOTHER,

Maria Garcia

Ever since she was editor of her high school yearbook, Sandra Garcia has been interested in putting words and images together. Working as an account executive for one of the nation's leading Hispanic advertising agencies, Bromley Communications, Sandra continues to pursue her interest in media and her love of Hispanic culture. ■ Sandra received her love of culture directly from her mother, Maria Garcia. Raised as a very proper young woman in Mexico, Maria discovered that she had to rely on her own strength and energy to tackle the many obstacles life put in her way. It is this strength and energy that drove her to become a U.S. citizen at sixty-one years of age, and which have become her legacy to her daughter.

WHEN MARIA GARCIA found out that she had passed her U.S. citizenship exam, she immediately called up her daughter Sandra at work. Both women screamed with joy. While citizenship may be something most people take for granted, to Sandra and her mother it couldn't have been a bigger deal. Sandra says that in the days after her mom took the test, she was a little nervous. "I wondered, what will happen if she fails?" She shouldn't have worried, because her mother has a gift for conquering situations that look impossible and making it all look easy.

Sandra remembers her mother as a constant blur of activity. "Even if she was in the house, my mom always moved around. She's always been very energetic, always active and always coming up with new things to do. She's very involved and she's always doing stuff. When she sees my sister and I relaxing and watching TV because it's been a hard week at work, she'll say, 'You're too young to be sitting there watching TV. Get up and live life.' She's so energetic that I always tell her that the minute that I hear her say that she's tired is the minute that I'm gonna worry because that's so not her."

Whether she was running across town selling Avon door-to-door or hosting a Tupperware party in her home, Sandra was always by her side. "Since I was the youngest one in the family, it was mandatory that I go with her, but eventually I grew to enjoy it. I remember her having a special bond with her mom as well."

Maria came from a big family and, like her daughter, was the one who was closest to her mother. Sandra's mother was born in Parmas, Mexico, but was raised in the city of Monterey, where some of her brothers and sisters still live. "My grandmother told us that our mom was the more reserved one," Sandra says. "She was the more obedient one, the easiest one to get along with, and the one that always wanted to be around her parents. She was no trouble at all."

As a teenager, Maria would frequently travel north from her home in Monterey, Mexico, to visit Laredo, Texas. "The cool thing to do back when she was young was to save your money and go shopping in Texas. It was a big thing to buy your clothes in the United States. She could do that because her older sister was living in San Antonio." On one of those visits to the States, her sister suggested that Maria go on a blind date with her brother-in-law. Maria reluctantly agreed to meet Rogelio.

A few days after their first meeting, Rogelio invited Maria to his sister's house for dinner. As he passed a bowl of food across the table, Rogelio casually remarked to his father that Maria was the woman he was going to marry. "Of course, my mom blushed and said, 'Oh my God, what did he say?' But my dad knew instantly that he was going to marry her."

The courtship took three years because Maria's mother was very strict and did not want to give her consent to the marriage. "It was very hard for my grandmother to let her daughter go and my mom struggled with it. Back then, if your parents didn't give you permission you wouldn't go through with it." But Rogelio was very persistent. "He took his uncle, he took his cousin, he took anyone he could think of to Mexico to convince them to let him marry their daughter. My grandfather finally told her, 'You are going to be twenty-seven years old. You're a woman. It's your life and you should do what you need to do.' But my mom still did not feel comfortable getting married without her mom's approval. After three years, my mom thought enough was enough and she eloped. So she left to join Rogelio, who was serving in the military in California."

While she finally had the church wedding she always wanted, it was unfortunately without her parents. "Even though she felt that she did the right thing, she always wished that her mom and dad could have been present at their wedding. The funny thing is that she couldn't get married without their help because she needed her birth certificate and her parents had it in Mexico. But her mom wouldn't give her the papers; my grandmother had them in a drawer and she wouldn't give them to anyone. One day, my grandfather sneaked out and stole the key and got my mom's birth certificate and papers and sent them to her in California. That's how she was able to have everything legal because her dad ended up helping her out."

Fortunately for Maria, after the wedding her mother accepted the marriage and her new son-in-law. "I think my grandmother was hurt and she couldn't believe that my mom would actually get married without her. But they had such a special relationship that I don't think my grandmother could have ever stayed angry for a long period of time."

The newlyweds lived in the San Diego area and soon had their first child. Maria, however, was uncomfortable with navigating an English-only world. "This was the time when we didn't have Spanish network television the way we do now. Back then she could only listen to Spanish music one hour a week on Sundays. She felt alienated and very homesick because she was so far away."

The family moved back to Texas, eventually settling in San Antonio. Though the Garcia family moved around following Rogelio's jobs, Maria's focus remained in one spot: her family. "She was always there for us in elementary school and in middle school because those were crucial years. She was waiting for all of us to be on our own so that she could go back and reevaluate what she wanted to do with her life."

According to her daughter, Maria has always been a focused and determined woman, doing whatever she has set her mind on. "She's always been very driven, but in terms of putting herself on some path that would lead her to some big prosperous career, she never did that. She's always talked about singing and she sings really well. She used to do some type of opera and her brother used to be in a mariachi band. I always wonder

Sandra Garcia and her mother,
Maria Garcia.

if she would have ever done anything with her singing if she had more time to focus on it instead of dedicating all of her time to her family."

When Sandra was fifteen her dad passed away unexpectedly. The tragedy that changed their family forever happened a week before Christmas during a festive family get-together. Sandra's brother and sister were home from college. "It was December sixteenth, 1989, I'll never forget. It was the Saturday right after the start of our Christmas vacation. We were cleaning the house and doing what we normally did. My mother's family arrived from Monterey and at some point we went to the mall, but my mom and my dad stayed behind. Twenty minutes after we left my dad just started coughing. He got up, drank his coffee, went to the rest room, and collapsed. And my mom had to deal with that all by herself because none of us were there.

"When we got back I remember getting to my house and it was really dark and there were a lot of cars outside and I thought, 'Oh, they probably invited more family and they're probably gonna have this big cookout.' Then one of my uncles approached me and told me that my dad had died. The level of shock that goes through you is huge. You're not expecting it; you don't even prepare for it. At that point all my mother could do was be worried about us. Even though he died with her alone she was worried about us."

A week after her father died, on Christmas Day, Maria and her family tried their best to make it a normal holiday, but it wasn't quite working. Then her mother began feeling sick. "We just thought that my mom was sad, because all of us were sad. But she called one of her sisters, who took her to the hospital because her blood pressure went up to some really dangerous level.

"So she was admitted to the hospital and of course my brother and my sister and I were like, 'Oh great, now it's my mom!' I couldn't believe it was happening. She was in the hospital a little less than a week, but she needed the time just to get some rest and let her body accept the fact that her mind was going through all of these emotions like a whirlwind. I remember telling her that nothing could happen to her because we still needed her. Of course that was very selfish of me, but she definitely said that was what was keeping her here. She knew she couldn't leave us without both our father and our mother. That was another super, super emotional time. We had just experienced my dad's death and then a week later, on Christmas Day, my mom was admitted to the hospital. But even then, when she was still in the hospital, she was strong. She told us all the things we needed to do and how we were supposed to behave and I was like, 'Yes, Mom, that's fine. Try to relax and take advantage of this time to recuperate as fast as you can.' And she did.

"Suddenly, at fifteen I was always worried about doing the right thing and being there for my mom. Even though she would encourage us to not worry, to be fearless and to live life and not dwell on things. She would say, 'You can't worry about things that you can't control.' That's one of the things I always try to remember. But it's easier said than done sometimes. Ever since my father's death, my mom has been this big pillar of strength for all of us. After going through that, we would always encourage each other. We told her, 'Mom, don't do the typical Mexican thing of wearing black for four years.' That is so customary in our culture. We told her, 'If you don't wear black, it doesn't mean that you didn't love Dad and you don't remember him.'

"She wore black for the funeral but I don't really remember how many months she wore black after that. She was sad for a while but it didn't seem like she dwelled on it. We were sad but we kept it very private. She would always say, 'Life goes on. You have to do what you have to do.' Two weeks after he died, I went back to school, my sister went back, and my brother went back. And my mom found stuff to keep her busy.

Maria practiced what she preached by never letting the little things stop her. Like her children, she moved on, becoming active in her church and joining three different choirs. "My mom likes to go out with her friends. Of course, her idea of going out is different from mine. She and her friends get together and pray the rosary."

Soon after the death of her father, Sandra and her family moved out of their house and moved in with her mother's sister. "I remember that was one of the hardest things for my mom to do because my mom was so independent and never wanted to bother people. I think a lot of it had to do with her pride. She wanted to do things on her own and she didn't want to feel like she needed other people's help. Moving in with my aunt was a huge deal for all of us. But as soon as the paperwork regarding my father's benefits was finished, my mom was ready to get out of there. She made a really wise choice because she wanted to secure her future as well. She told us she was going to buy herself a house. Even if she could only buy herself a little house, she was gonna pay for it in full so that she knew that she would always have her own home and wouldn't ever need to depend on anyone again. She bought herself that little house, and to this day, she still has the same little house. It's paid for in full. She bought a car and my brother learned how to drive and we used that car for a long, long time. She provided security for herself and her family."

While Maria made sure that her future was secure, she also taught her daughter to be concerned about the security of others. "I had lots of very vivid memories of my mom being very friendly and very helpful to people in need. I remember on a bus trip from Monterey to San Antonio, my mother started talking to a couple from Mexico. They had a baby and they told my mom that their car had broken down, which was why they were taking the bus. My mom always strikes up conversations very easily with people. So she saw the baby and she started talking to the lady. My mom discovered that these people really needed some help. They didn't have a lot of money, their car had broken down, and they didn't know anyone in San Antonio. So my mom offered them her house. I was like, 'What are you doing? We don't even know who these people are.' And she said, 'I have a good feeling. And you never know. What if that was you and your brother and something happened to you? I would want someone to extend their home to you, too.' These people were desperate and planned to stay in the Greyhound station. My mom said, 'No, you can't do that, you have a baby. Come to our house, you're more than welcome.' And even the people couldn't believe that my mom was doing this. But sure enough, they stayed in our house one night and they were very, very, very thankful. They just kept on telling my mom, 'Your help will never be forgotten. If you ever go to Mexico City, please call us. You were like an angel to us. You don't even know who we are.' They were just super, super, super grateful.

"And that just struck me. You grow up hearing, 'Don't talk to strangers.' You're not supposed to do what my mom did, invite total strangers to your house and let them sleep there and eat there and see everything that you have. Not that we had a lot, but my mom was a widow, so it was not like she had her husband there in case she needed him for protection. It was just her and my sister and myself. My sister and I couldn't believe she did that, but then we were so proud that she did it. I think she even lent them money to go back. At one point when my mom went to Mexico City, she saw the couple and they were like, 'Oh, all of my family knows about you! We always tell them about the lady we met in San Antonio!' My mom always did stuff like that. I would say, 'Mom, it's not like they're gonna pay you back, you don't even know who they are.' But she would do it."

The courage that it took for Maria to extend herself to

strangers is based on an unshakable confidence in herself. She knew who she was as a Latina and stressed the importance of that knowledge to her children as well. "My mom always taught me to be very proud of the fact that I could speak both Spanish and English. Of course she always spoke in Spanish, but she always emphasized that we should speak English as well. She said, 'You watch, it's gonna be very helpful, you're gonna be able to get great jobs because you can do both and you can do them well. She always wanted us to watch Spanish TV and to appreciate Spanish music and all its variations. So I knew from being very little that I wanted to do something that focused on the Latino culture, something that would surround me with the culture. I just happened to land into advertising because I was a communication-arts student, focusing on production. One of my classes took a tour of the local advertising agency, which happened to be the number-one Hispanic advertising agency in the nation. I fell in love with the agency and with advertising as well. I did an internship and I've been working here for over four years. But I always think of other things to do that keep me close to the community because I've always enjoyed it."

While her daughter makes her mark in the world of advertising, Maria has decided to make some marks of her own. At sixty-one years of age, Sandra's mother finally decided to apply for her U.S. citizenship. "Talk about procrastination! I think she's figured she's been here so long she can't believe she hasn't done it before now. Sometimes she said she didn't do it because she didn't have the money, but we know it's not expensive. It's not like it's millions of dollars or even thousands of dollars. Realizing that she's lived longer in the United States than she ever did in Mexico, she probably feels entitled and wants to be part of the process. We don't really talk about voting and stuff like that, but I saw how hard she studied the questionnaires, so it's important to her. I saw her studying her questions and it's kind of funny to see your mom at sixty-one trying to study about the Bill of Rights or trying to remember the names of the first thirteen colonies. She asked me to quiz her and when she got the answers right, she said, 'You see, I'm smart. I told you I'm smart.' She finally took the exam and when she went through the interview, her interviewer told her she was 'outstanding' and she passed.

"The whole experience is funny in a way because I can't believe that it's actually happened. But it's also inspiring because she still doesn't dominate the English language, but she certainly knows it a lot better than when she first came. She has never said, 'Oh, I'm too old to learn. I'm too old to study these questions. I'll never get them right.' No, she said, 'Hey, can you go on the Internet and print me the questions so I can study?' "

Sandra plans to get the entire family together to celebrate when Maria goes through her citizenship ceremony. Her brother will fly into Texas from California and the three Garcia children will toast their mother on her latest achievement. Sandra says, "It's a big deal. Her whole idea of never being too old to learn is inspiring." ■